C2 083518 99

C000141128

This book is to be returned on
the last date stamped below.

07 13. MAY 87   26. NOV 87   08. MAR 89.

2   4ᵗʰ June 87   28. JAN. 1988   09. MAY 89.

    18. AUG 87   14. MAR 88

    18. AUG 87   25. MAY 88   -5. JUL 1989

22.   29. AUG 88   24. OCT 89.
    24. OCT 87   25. NOV 89

DUNFERMLINE DISTRICT LIBRARIES
Central Library
Abbot Street
Dunfermline

08. APR 87   09. SEP 88

QUILTING: PATCHWORK & TRAPUNTO

By Linda S. Weeks
and Jo Ippolito Christensen

Sterling Publishing Co., Inc.   New York

Photographs by Marcus Dillon, Jr., and Bob Weeks
Drawings by Susan Henderson and Nancy Hom

CE

C2083518 99

746.46

REQ.

Second Printing, 1981
"Quilting: Patchwork & Trapunto"
Copyright © 1980 by Sterling Publishing Co., Inc.
Two Park Avenue, New York, N.Y. 10016
is a combined edition of
"Patchwork & other Quilting" © 1973 by Sterling Publishing Co., Inc. and
"Trapunto: Decorative Quilting" © 1972 by Sterling Publishing Co., Inc.
Distributed in Australia by Oak Tree Press Co., Ltd.
P.O. Box J34 Brickfield Hill, Sydney 2000 N.S.W.
Distributed in the United Kingdom by Oak Tree Press Ltd. U.K.
Available in Canada from Oak Tree Press Ltd.
% Canadian Manda Group, 215 Lakeshore Boulevard East
Toronto, Ontario M5A 3W9
Manufactured in the United States of America
All rights reserved
Library of Congress Catalog Card No.: 80-51925
Sterling ISBN 0-8069-8930-0

Contents

PATCHWORK

Before You Begin Patchworking

Whoever said that quilting is only for people with lots of time to spare could not have been more wrong. Quilting is for everyone—young and old, men and women, career girls and housewives. Any quilt that *you* design and quilt is something to treasure and be proud of. Do not let the opportunity to make your own hand-made quilt pass because you feel harried or do not know how to start. Making a quilt requires only basic sewing skills, yet the finished product is satisfying and beautiful and certainly original.

Quilting is a two-part process. First you choose a top piece or a pattern, which you can design and piece together according to the instructions in this book. Then you quilt the designed part to another piece of material, with a layer of filling in between. The pattern of the quilting stitches is as important a part of your quilt as is the design itself.

To get the feel of quilting, thumb through this book and look at the different patterns. Better yet, if there is someone you know who owns some quilts, take a look at a real quilt, not just a picture, and see what it feels like and how beautiful the stitchery can be. When you decide on a pattern, start looking for the right material or rummage through sewing scraps and pick out pieces of material with special meaning. Because each quilt is hand-made, you add your personal touch to any pattern, and the result, of course, is a very personal quilt. For example, you can alter the Lone Star on page 25 in hundreds of ways by simply changing the combination of colors in making the star.

If you need a reason to begin, other than for the pleasure of making your own quilt, think of giving a quilt the next time you need a special present for a new bride or a new family addition. Generations ago, American girls were not only expected to have completed a number of quilts for their own home linens before marrying, but women and friends of the community got together and quilted a bridal or wedding quilt for the new bride. Often, showers were given for the bride, and each guest brought a quilt block, which the bride put together and then invited the guests to a quilting bee. Also, any new mother would be proud to have a special baby quilt for her new-born—and there is a special section in this book on baby and infant quilts.

Most experienced quilters are only too glad to help a novice. If you have any questions, they would probably be glad to help. In fact, why not consider the revival of the community quilting bee?

Materials

Materials for quilting are inexpensive and readily available in most homes. The only item a new quilter might have to purchase is a quilting frame and even this is easy to construct if you are at all talented with a saw and drill. See Illus. 1 for a do-it-yourself frame. Purchase what is called 1 × 2 inch lumber and cut it to your size specifications (see page 18 for instructions on determining your quilt size). Cut two strips the length you want your longest quilt, and two

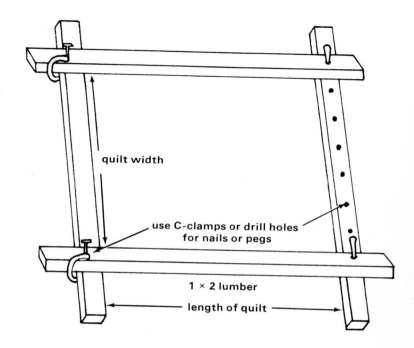

Illus. 1. To make your own frame, use four pieces of what is called 1 × 2 inch lumber. To join the wood into a frame, either drill holes at 2- or 3-inch intervals, as shown on the right, or use C-clamps, as shown on the left.

quilt width

use C-clamps or drill holes for nails or pegs

1 × 2 lumber

length of quilt

strips to equal the quilt width (plus an extra 6 inches for tacking room). Drill holes at 2- or 3-inch intervals if you plan to use nails or pegs to hold the quilt frame intact, or eliminate the drilling and use C-clamps, as shown.

It is a good idea to organize a quilting box in which you can keep several needles of the same size, some adhesive tape to protect your fingertips from needle pricks, and a couple of thimbles. If you are not accustomed to wearing a thimble,

now is the time to learn, for it is almost impossible to quilt without one.

Most quilters recommend using a short, sharp needle (No. 8 or 9) for quilting and a longer needle for piecing tops. When you have completed your first quilt, you will notice that your needle has developed a slight curvature and is easier to use. With this initiation completed, your needle is an official quilting needle. Some quilters think needles should be sold with a curvature, but purists believe each hand must break in its own needle.

In the past, Number 30 quilting thread was always used for the quilting stitch, but today many quilters prefer to use a 40 or 50 thread, as it makes a finer stitch. The new polyester threads are much more durable than their earlier equivalents, and there is little problem with this new thread breaking easily. Always be on guard, however, for a faulty spool of thread. If your thread has a tendency to break easily, get a new spool. The color thread you use depends on your own quilt and personal taste.

In addition to the tools for quilting, you need to buy batting or filling for each quilt. This is, as its name implies, the middle layer or filling in the quilt. Until recently, quilters used cotton batting exclusively. Before processed batting was available, they even made their own batting from samples from local cotton gins. Now, however, there are several excellent synthetic blend fillings on the market. The new fillings seem to launder better than the cotton ones, because they are lighter and fluffier. Some people still prefer cotton batting, however, and if you decide to use the cotton be sure to purchase white cotton—and not the brown variety—in a single roll. These batting rolls are available in various sizes so check the measurements on the package to be sure the roll will fit your quilt.

Before you can use all these materials, you must have a quilt to quilt.

A Simple Quilt

A quilt is composed of three layers—a top, which is usually pieced or patterned in some way, the batting or filler, and the backing, also called the lining. Quilting is the process of holding these three layers of material together. The quilt backing must be cut or pieced to equal the dimensions of the quilt top. This backing should be the same type material as the quilt top and can be any color or print, although it should match or complement the quilt top. Fine white muslin or cotton is often used for backing material because it is easy to quilt, inexpensive, and looks quite nice when finished.

To become acquainted with the quilting process, buy two permanent press sheets or two pieces of permanent press material, perhaps a print for the top piece and a matching or complementary solid for the backing. Do not concern yourself yet with intricate patchwork or appliqué patterns. Instead, concentrate first on learning how to prepare your layers for quilting and then on doing the actual quilting. You can dream up and design original patterns and designs when you are familiar with what quilting itself is.

Stretching the Quilt in the Frame

To place your quilt in the frame, first thumbtack one side of the backing to the frame, spacing the thumbtacks about 3 inches apart. Gently pull the material across the frame and tack the other side. Do not worry about pulling the material taut at this time. When you have tacked the two sides onto the frame, tack the ends in the same manner.

Illus. 2. First thumbtack the backing to the frame. After you have tacked all four sides, loosen the C-clamps and gently pull the frame out to tighten the backing.

After all four sides are tacked in place, have someone help you loosen the C-clamps on two corners and pull the frame out, thereby stretching and tightening the backing. Do not pull the frames too tight, or you will tear the material.

With the backing in place, you can smooth the batting over it. Be careful not to pull holes in the batting when you unroll and stretch it. To stretch the batting over the back, slide your hand under it and gently smooth it outward. Always leave

Illus. 3. Once the backing is in place, smooth batting over it, leaving several inches of the backing uncovered.

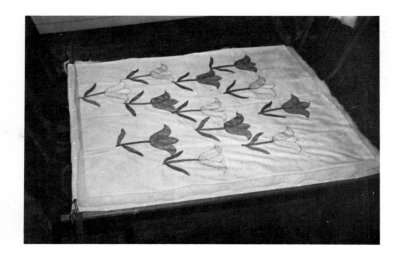

Illus. 4. When the batting is smooth, carefully place the top so it completely covers the batting.

several inches on each side of the backing free for the quilt hem.

Make sure your batting is smooth and wrinkle free, then spread the top over it. The top should completely cover the batting. When all three layers are in place, baste them together along all four sides.

If you are using a quilting hoop and not a frame,

Illus. 5. Baste all three layers in place.

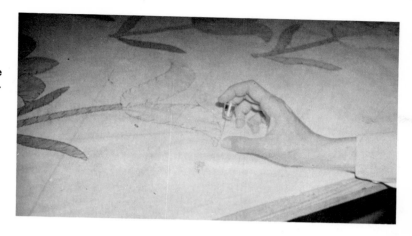

Illus. 6. Your hands should be in this position while you quilt.

follow the same directions, but instead of tacking the quilt into the frame, lay it out on the floor or a table and place all three layers together. Baste the three layers together along all four sides but place additional basting lines through the middle of the quilt to avoid wrinkles when you change the position of the hoop.

Quilting Stitch

Finally, you are ready to quilt. The actual quilting is the most time-consuming of all the steps in making a quilt, but, with a little practice, quilting becomes easy and relaxing. The purpose of quilting is to hold the three layers of the quilt together, and only as early quilters became more concerned with the beauty of their craft did they perfect the beautiful quilting designs we have today.

You do, indeed, plan the quilting pattern with the top pattern of the quilt in mind, as the secondary purpose of the quilting stitch is to enhance the design in the fabric or the pieced or appliquéd pattern you have worked so hard to make. It is recommended, therefore, that you emphasize quilting in plain areas and play down quilting stitches in patterned areas.

Most quilt top patterns will, by their design, dictate where you should quilt. You have, however, much liberty in choosing patterns for borders and strips, but keep in mind the type of quilt top pattern you have for the over-all quilt top. A geometric border might look out of place with a dainty appliqué top and a scroll border will not match a bold geometric quilt top. As with materials, keep like designs together.

If you choose an elaborate pattern, sketch the entire design onto the quilt with pencil or marking chalk before you begin quilting. Some quilting companies even sell pattern perforations in which you rub over the cut patterns with chalk dust. Always use a material for marking that will wash off easily.

The quilting stitch is a very fine running stitch. By holding your needle at an acute angle, you can punch it down and then back up near the same point. When you are experienced with this stitch, you can take several stitches on the needle before pulling the thread through the quilt. A good measure is to make 5 to 9 stitches per inch, depending on the thickness of the quilt. Try to achieve uniform stitches rather than small stitches at first.

To begin quilting, knot the end of the thread you have chosen (see page 8). Bring the needle up through the quilt and pull the knot through the backing so it is embedded in the filling or batting. This eliminates unsightly knots on the quilt back. To end off your stitch, make a simple backstitch and run the thread through the filling.

As the quilting progresses in the framed method, remove the thumbtacks and roll the quilt up gradually. As you quilt each section with the hoop, you gradually move out towards the quilt edges.

You may quilt on a sewing machine if you do not have time or space to set up a frame or if you are interested in making a lovely quilt not of a hand-made quality. Machine-quilt with a straight stitch, and a stitch length between 6 and 12 per inch. Adjust the tension according to the thickness before sewing the actual quilt. Machine-quilting yields a uniform stitch and makes quilting possible for many people who would never before have tried it.

Illus. 7. Close-up of the quilting stitch.

Finishing the Edges

When you have completed the quilting, remove the quilt from the frame. Depending on the quilt's pattern and style, there are several ways in which you can finish it. The most common method is to fold the backing over the top about 1 inch, turn it under and slip stitch it down. This simple method makes a nice finished edge that holds up well. If

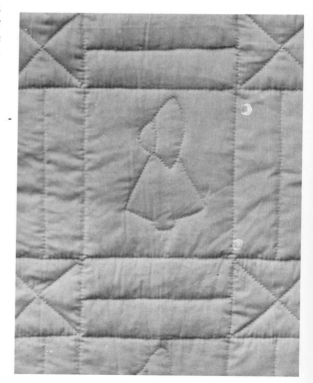

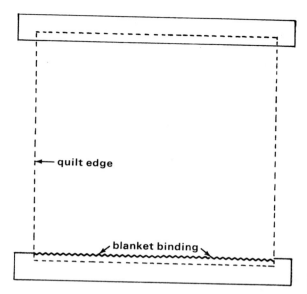

you hem by hand, use a single thread and make the stitches as invisible as possible. If the backing is a print that would not make an attractive small border on the quilt, you can roll a small piece of the front border to the quilt back and stitch it down in the same manner.

Another possible edge for a quilt is blanket binding, either satin or cotton, which you can sew round the edges of the quilt. Cut two strips of blanket binding, which you can buy in sewing supply shops, each one the length of the quilt ends plus twice the width of the binding itself. If the quilt is 36 inches and the binding is 3 inches, for example, cut the strips 42 inches long. Place the binding at least one inch overlapping the quilt edge and zig-zag stitch (see Illus. 8).

Now cut binding for the quilt sides, measuring the binding for each side the length of the quilt plus twice the width of the binding. Zig-zag stitch this length of binding in place, leaving the ends covering the width binding free (see Illus. 9).

Cut the strips you have just sewn on the quilt sides on a diagonal at the ends, giving the binding a mitered effect. Turn the cut edges under and zig-zag stitch securely (see Illus. 10).

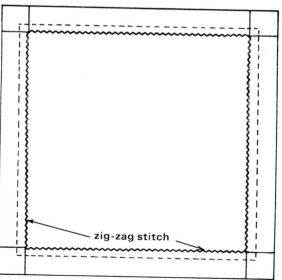

Illus. 9. Cut binding for the sides. Then zig-zag stitch the binding as shown.

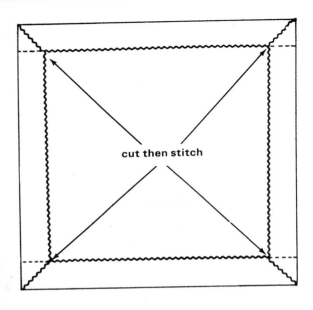

cut then stitch

Illus. 10. Cut the strips at the corners you have left open. Then zig-zag stitch them in place.

For a more elaborate edging or if you plan to use the quilt as a coverlet on a bed top, you can sew ruffles or fringe round the edge.

Some quilts require bias tape or quilt binding to finish the edges. One pattern that often requires such finishing is the flower garden quilt (see page 31), because the edge is scalloped. It is simpler and neater to sew quilt binding or bias tape onto such scalloped edges. You can, however, use bias tape, particularly colored bias tape, to create a contrast, on the edges of any quilt.

Baby quilts have a special finished look if you add satin blanket binding round the edges. Also, ruffles often decorate these small quilts nicely.

The final choice of an edging is up to you, but remember to keep the quilt material in mind when you choose the edging material.

Now that you are familiar with how to quilt, you are ready to begin designing your own quilt tops. Because the process of quilting—setting up the frame, tacking the layers to the frame, drawing on a quilting pattern and stitching—is usually more or less the same, the rest of this book will mostly be concerned with actual quilt patterns. It is taken for granted that after you design and piece the quilt top, you will choose an appropriate backing, stretch and tack it and the other two layers to the frame, quilt it, and attractively finish off the edges.

The Art of Patchwork

Patchwork quilts have been known since American colonial women stitched scraps of used clothing into bedcovers and filled them with grasses and corn husks. These early quilts were not held together with the beautiful quilting stitch we know today, but rather were tied at intervals with twine. Colonial life afforded some leisure time, and the women took pride in the making of quilts. Although quilters were forced to use small scraps of material, making new patterns became a challenge and women took pleasure in inventing patchwork designs. They developed lovely quilting patterns to decorate their patchwork or pieced tops and to hold them together. Cotton was used as a filler for the quilts.

If you hear names such as Turkey Tracks,

Illus. 11. This is only one of innumerable patchwork designs that you can create. Choose a specific pattern, or sew your patches in any decorative, abstract fashion.

Illus. 12. A nine-patch pattern.

Illus. 13. A variation of the nine-patch pattern.

Bluebirds for Happiness, Philadelphia Pavements, Jacob's Ladder or Hole in the Barn Door, you can guess where the inspiration for many patterns comes from. Early quilters took cues from the sources around them and in many early quilts birds, animals, plants and religious themes are the most prevalent. Many years before women were allowed to vote, they showed their political bias in their needlework. Presidential elections brought forth such new pattern names as Washington's Quilt, Lincoln's Platform, Jackson's Star and Democrat Rose.

Many popular patterns are known by several different names and a new member of a quilting circle might be easily confused. There are several reasons for this name problem: If a quilt was brought into a new area with a name that someone had already used, the first name was simply dropped and a new name picked. Or, perhaps a quilter took a new pattern home with her after visiting another area and simply forgot the original name, so she just re-named the pattern. In some cases, names were mispronounced or misunderstood as the pattern travelled from area to area and a new name was born.

Today's quilter has literally hundreds of patterns to choose from when making a quilt. However, for the beginning quilter, one of the simpler patterns, like a four-patch or nine-patch would be a good start. As you gain skill in your piecing and

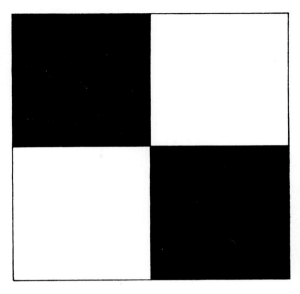

Illus. 14. For your first quilt, try a simple four-patch pattern, which is not difficult and is very attractive.

uilting ability, you can select a more complicated attern.

A patchwork or pieced quilt is made by cutting mall squares, triangles, hexagons or diamonds— rst from a cardboard or sandpaper pattern and nen from fabric—and piecing them together to orm a large block or an over-all design. The main eature of the patchwork quilt is not the pattern ut rather the colors that make up the pattern. arly quilters had an excellent eye for color and nany old quilts are now on display in museums or their designs painted with needle and thread. ven a simple four-patch quilt can be beautiful if ou carefully plan color combinations. As a rule f thumb for color selection, before sewing a quilt ogether, lay it out to see how the colors react to nd complement each other.

A well made quilt is a thing of beauty, but it nust also be durable. *Always* use new material— his is the most important thing to remember in iecing a quilt. The material can be sewing scraps r fabric you purchase especially for quilt pieces. t is always a good idea to test the fabric by vashing and ironing a small piece before you ut out the quilt pieces. If the sample piece fades r shrinks, it is better to pre-shrink all the material ather than ruin the entire quilt. Keep in mind as ou select the material the type of quilt you are naking and the use the quilt will receive. Cotton, inen, fine muslin, corduroy and the new cotton lends are excellent material choices, especially ince you can launder the finished quilt at home.

Square-Patch Quilts

The simple four-patch pattern is an excellent starter quilt. This pattern is made up of four squares of two contrasting colors which together form a larger block. As many blocks as necessary for any specific bed size make up the entire quilt top. To determine the quilt size, measure the bed for which you are making your quilt to get the exact size. The quilt should cover the mattress top and hang over as far as you like. If you plan to use the quilt as a blanket, allow extra room on the sides to cover a sleeping person. Allow 17 inches, or more, if the quilt is to cover the pillows on the bed, in addition to extra yardage for the foot of the bed. (See Illus. 15.)

The size of your individual squares depends on the over-all size of your quilt, but a 4-inch square

17

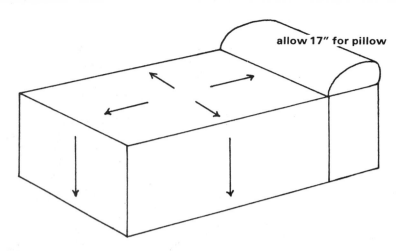

allow 17" for pillow

Illus. 15. To determine the size
make your quilt, measure
dimensions of the bed. Add ext
for a person, if you are making
blanket, or the pillow, if you a
making a bedspread.

is a good size with which to begin working.
Blocks smaller than 4 inches are difficult to work
with and those larger than 5 or 6 inches become
unwieldy for the beginner. When you decide on
the block size, enlarge it $\frac{1}{2}$ inch to allow for seams,
then cut several squares from cardboard or sandpaper. (For example, for a finished block that is
4 inches, cut patterns $4\frac{1}{2}$ inches.) Press all material
you will use to eliminate wrinkles, then lay the
cardboard pattern on the material and trace round
it with a pencil or marking chalk. Be sure the
pattern follows the grain of the material. Since
cutting is one of the most important steps in
making a quilt, use sharp scissors and trace your
pattern carefully. When all your patches are cut,
divide them according to color or design and
either string them together with a single thread
through the center, or keep them in a small,
convenient box.

Since this particular pattern is usually ma
from scrap material, no yardage requirements a
given. However, if, for example, you want
finished quilt 60 × 72 inches, you divide yo
4-inch blocks into 60 and 72 and determine th
you need a total of 15 blocks across and 18 bloc
lengthwise. Since these blocks are in so
of two's, you divide 2 units into 18 and fin
that you need 9 sets down. When you divi
2 units into 15, you find that you need $7\frac{1}{2}$ uni
across. Ignore the $\frac{1}{2}$ unit for now, and work wi
7 across. You can make up the 4 inches short
60 on the sides when you hem the quilt. Yo
will have a finished quilt of 56 (7 sets × 2 units
4 inches) × 72 (9 sets × 2 units × 4 inche
Cut a total of 252 (14 × 18), $4\frac{1}{2}$-inch squares f
this particular quilt.

A good color combination to keep in mind f
the four-patch quilt is dark and light colors t

gether and possibly prints and solids together. Choose colors to match a specific room's décor.

You can piece a quilt at your leisure—while talking with friends, waiting at the doctor's office or when you take time out from your job, schoolwork or household chores. If you have cut all your squares beforehand, you can piece blocks gradually, then set them together after you have completed sewing. If piecing by hand, use a simple running stitch to sew pieces together, but be sure to finish off stitches by backstitching several times so the threads will not pull out. Many quilters today prefer to machine-stitch block patterns, claiming that the machine stitches hold much

Illus. 17. This baby quilt shows one of many star designs you can make. See page 25 for star instructions.

Illus. 16. This is one possible patchwork design you can follow.

better and are quicker to make. This is a personal preference depending on whether you want to sit down at a machine or quietly work on your quilt in your spare time. Whichever method you choose, simply place right sides of the material together and stitch at least a $\frac{1}{8}$-inch seam. The seam size is not as important as making sure all seams are uniform.

For the four-patch pattern, piece the blocks in halves, then sew the halves together. When you have pieced all the blocks, sew the halves together. When all the blocks have been pieced, you can sew them together for the final quilt size or

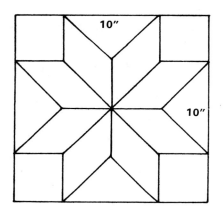

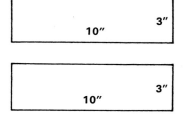

3" square

Illus. 18. Cut strips which are the length and width of your squares, and center blocks to piece at the corners.

you can set them together with strips as shown in Illus. 18 and 19. Illus. 21 is a quilt which has been joined together by strips.

Setting a quilt together in this way is not difficult. If a block is 10 inches square, for example, cut strips the same length, and whatever width you need to obtain your finished quilt size. You must also cut small center blocks the same size as the strip width (see Illus. 18). If the blocks are not square, the measurements of the strips and squares will vary accordingly.

After you have cut all the strips and squares, sew the strips to the block sides, completing one line across the quilt (see Illus. 19). When you have joined these strips and blocks, sew all the bottom blocks together as pictured in Illus. 19. Then sew these two strips together, keeping right sides together as you sew. You may edge the quilt

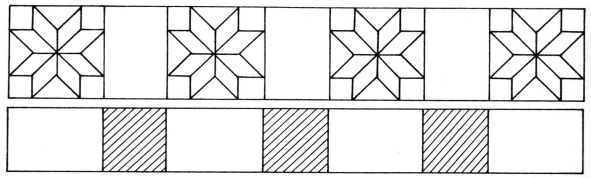

Illus. 19. Sew the strips to the patchwork blocks, with right sides together, to complete one row. Then join the strips to the center blocks for another row. Join the rows together and continue in this manner to complete the quilt top.

with a border the same width as the strips, as in Illus. 21.

If you enjoy piecing quilts but do not want to spend the time to hand-quilt them, try machine-quilting. You can do this with or without a quilting foot on the machine. The only difficulty you might have is keeping the material straight and avoiding puckers. Otherwise, tack your pieced quilt to your frame, and quilt as instructed on page 11.

If, perhaps, you do not want to hand- or machine-quilt, look around or place an ad in the local newspaper for a person who quilts. There may be someone in your area who will do extra quilting, and would be eager to quilt for you.

Illus. 21. This lovely patchwork quilt was pieced and then set together with strips as described on page 20.

Illus. 20 (above). This simple variation of a four-patch pattern is entitled Shoofly.

Illus. 22 (right). Broken Dishes is the name of this four-patch variation.

Bow-Tie Quilt

Many interesting patchwork patterns have been developed from the basic square and one of these, with a slight variation, is the Bow-Tie or Neck-Tie Quilt, shown in Illus. 23. This quilt pattern is extremely versatile and a good example of how color combinations can change the entire look of a quilt.

The bow-tie itself is a four-square block with a small square in the middle which cuts the corners of the larger squares. Cut the middle square and two diagonal squares from the same material, thereby giving the appearance of a bow-tie. Cut the other two squares in the block from a contrasting or matched solid color or a print (see Illus. 24 for the pattern).

This quilt is simple to piece. As for the plain four-patch quilt, you can piece each bow block separately and then set all the blocks together. Since the pattern is usually pieced together from assorted material scraps, specific color combina-

Illus. 23. Patchwork designs are sometimes based round specific motifs. This pattern, as you can see, is based on a bow-tie shape.

Illus. 24. Pattern pieces for the Bow-Tie Quilt.

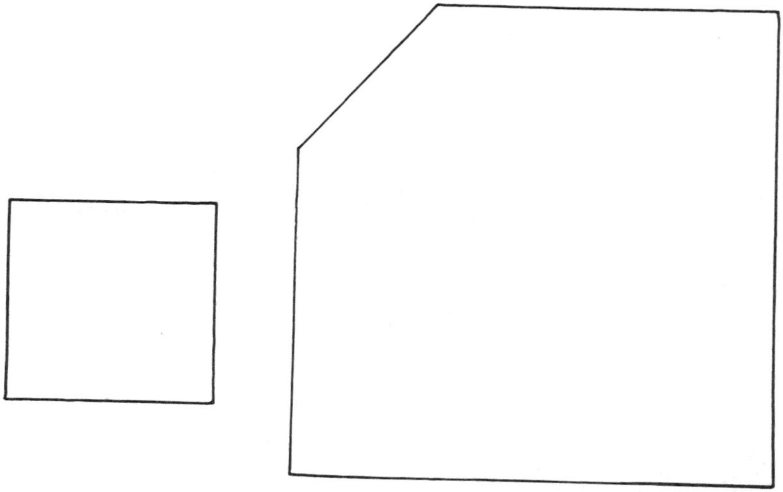

tions or yardage requirements are not given. If you do want to purchase special fabric for the pattern, follow this simple estimating method: decide what size you would like your individual squares to be, then figure how many you will need to make the quilt its finished size. Then, estimate how many of these blocks you can cut from $\frac{1}{2}$ yard of material and buy your material to equal all the blocks you need.

With right sides together, piece the three sections together that form the bow-tie, and then piece the other two blocks to the tie. With white thread (unless you are using very dark material) sew the blocks together with $\frac{1}{4}$-inch seams. These blocks are not usually set together with strips, but if you would like to do so, simply figure the width and length of each strip and sew the strips with a $\frac{1}{4}$-inch stitch to the bow-tie blocks.

Illus. 25. This is the Lone Star Quilt whose directions begin on page 25.

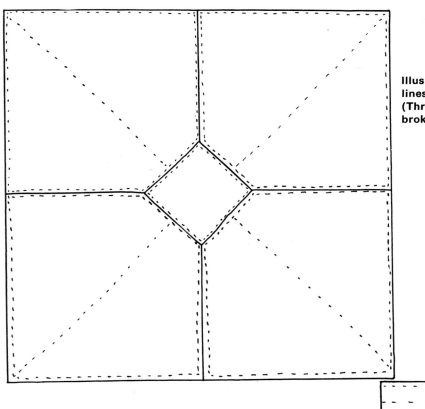

Illus. 26. Suggested quiltin
lines for the Bow-Tie Qui
(Throughout this book, straig
broken lines indicate quiltin
lines.)

Quilt along the edge of each piece so the bow-tie pattern is reversed on the quilt back. Or, see the quilting suggestion in Illus. 27 for another possible pattern for the quilting lines.

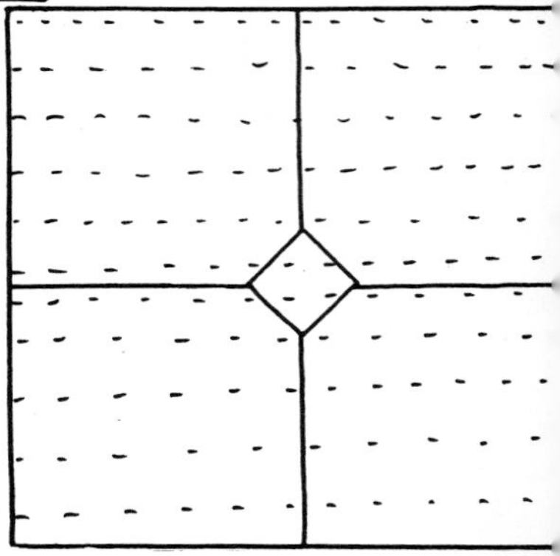

Illus. 27. Another possible quilting pattern for the Bow-Tie Quilt.

Lone Star Quilt

One of the most popular of all American motifs in quilt patterns is the star, of which there are more than 100 pattern variations. A very common pattern is the Lone Star Quilt, known in some areas as the Rising Sun and Star of the West. Whichever of these names you have heard, the pattern is probably the same: small diamonds pieced together to make eight identical sections which are joined for the large eight-point star. In addition to the large middle star, many Lone Star quilts have smaller stars and half stars appliquéd to the background. The Lone Star is classified as a masterpiece quilt because it is intricate, but if you cut your pattern carefully and sew evenly you should have no trouble piecing this beautiful quilt.

First select colors for the quilt. Lay all colors out in some pattern and notice their over-all effect. Experiment with new and bold colors and try some new combinations. Lavender and yellow make a lovely combination, as do orange and blue in subtle tones. This pattern is basically the same in all designs and if you find a particular color combination you prefer, simply use this diamond pattern and follow the general directions to make your pattern.

Because the finished size of this quilt depends on the size border you use in the pattern, you can make the completed quilt larger or smaller than the suggested finished size. If you follow the diamond pattern in Illus. 28 and add a border of $5\frac{3}{4}$ inches on the sides and 8 inches on the top and bottom, the finished quilt should be approximately 87 inches long and 77 inches wide. However, by adding more diamonds in the piecing order given, or by adding a wider border, you can enlarge the quilt. To make a smaller quilt, simply use a smaller diamond pattern.

To make the quilt shown in Illus. 25, you need the following material: $\frac{1}{4}$ yard of dark purple for the 8 middle diamonds; $\frac{1}{2}$ yard or less each, depending on the width of material, for the 16 medium purple and for the 24 light purple diamonds; $1\frac{1}{2}$ yards of material for the 72 dark pink diamonds; 1 yard of red for the 48 red diamonds; 1 yard each of medium pink and light pink; $\frac{1}{2}$ yard of yellow and light green, and $\frac{1}{4}$ yard of dark green.

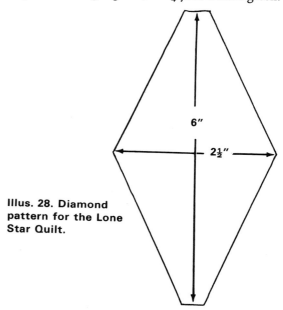

Illus. 28. Diamond pattern for the Lone Star Quilt.

6″

2½″

Illus. 30. A baby quilt is a wonderful gift for any newborn child. Because the size is often relatively small, you can design and create a baby quilt faster than most full-sized quilts.

Illus. 29. Many simple, but decorative, motifs make charming appliqués. This señorita, appliquéd to a complementary background, is a lively figure to adorn a quilt.

Illus. 31. This is another possible cradle quilt you can make.

Illus. 33. Flowers lend themselves well to appliquéd quilts. This is a dahlia, but you can choose any flower you like.

Illus. 32. Appliqués need not be exact imitations of natural colors. These patterned butterflies certainly are not true-to-life, but are, nevertheless, attractive motifs for a quilt.

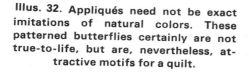

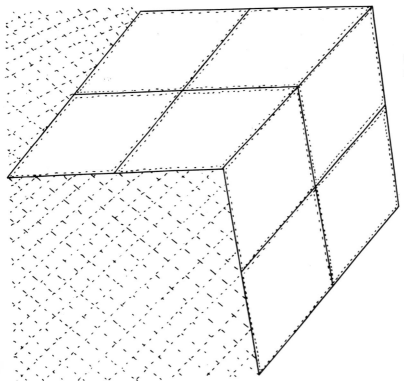

Cut 40 medium pink diamonds, 32 light pink, 24 yellow, 16 light green and 8 dark green.

The star consists of eight diamond-shaped sections, each section a parallelogram with six rows of six diamonds. To make the first star section, piece diamonds together in the following order: dark purple, medium purple, light purple, two rows of dark pink, red. Piece the second row starting with medium purple and ending with medium pink. Begin the third row with light purple and end with light pink. Continue piecing in this manner until you have pieced all six rows. Sew the rows together to form a parallelogram.

When you have completed the first section, make seven more following the same directions. Having all dark purple points in the center, join four sections to make half of the star and then the other four sections for the other half. Join the two halves to finish the eight-point star.

After completing the star, measure the distance

between the points on the star and cut six squares of background material (you will need four or five yards of this background material) to fit into the corner squares on the star. Cut two of the squares in half diagonally so you have four triangles. Sew the squares and triangles to the star as shown in Illus. 25.

Using any color scrap material left from the large star, cut enough diamonds to make four whole stars and four half stars. Sew the diamonds together and turn the small star edges under. Appliqué the whole stars to the squares and the half stars to the triangles as shown in Illus. 25. (See page 35 for instructions on the appliqué stitches.)

You need approximately $7\frac{1}{2}$ yards of material

for the backing and the border of the quilt. In the photograph of the Lone Star, the backing material is white, as is the filler between star points, and the border is the yellow in the large star. You may, however, use a print material for the back and a solid from the star for the border. A border 8 to 10 inches wide would look nice on this quilt, but you may use a larger border to increase the quilt size. Cut four border strips, piece them together and stitch them around the top of the quilt using $\frac{1}{4}$-inch seams.

The Lone Star quilt is usually quilted according to the pattern in Illus. 34. However, you can choose any quilting pattern you want for the border. It is recommended that the thread for the quilting match the backing material.

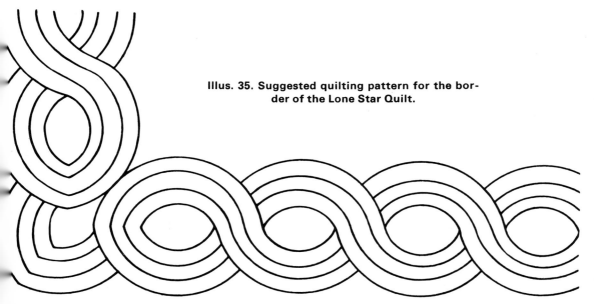

Illus. 35. Suggested quilting pattern for the border of the Lone Star Quilt.

Illus. 36. This Rose Quilt is a lovely addition in any bedroom, living room or den. The design is simple, but the effect striking if you choose attractive colors. Refer to pages 42 and 43 for instructions and patterns.

Illus. 37. Overall Sam is a fun quilt to design, because you have unlimited choice in dressing him. You can use different scraps for the overalls and shirt of each figure on the quilt. See pages 40 and 41 for instructions and patterns.

Grandmother's Flower Garden Quilt

Often, quilts can serve as remembrances of special events or motifs. A century and more ago, Presentation quilts were very popular. Women of the community worked on individual blocks, pieced and quilted them and then presented the quilt to a special friend or, more commonly, to a visiting dignitary.

Like many other quilts, this one is known by several names—Martha Washington's Garden, The Mosaic, The Hexagon, or The Honeycomb. The important difference when it is called a "garden" quilt, whether it is Martha Washington's or Grandmother's, is that each flower is surrounded by a row of green to represent flower leaves and then a row of white to represent the winding path through the garden.

Grandmother's Flower Garden Quilt is a beautiful quilt and is considered, by many, a treasure to own. It is a difficult quilt to piece and you must do it with care and precision. When you have finished, however, you will certainly consider it one of the best quilts in your collection.

Illus. 38. Usually Grandmother's Flower Garden Quilt has a definite order of colors. Although this variation does follow the traditional pattern, however, the colors are totally different. You can, of course, choose any colors to suit your particular needs and taste.

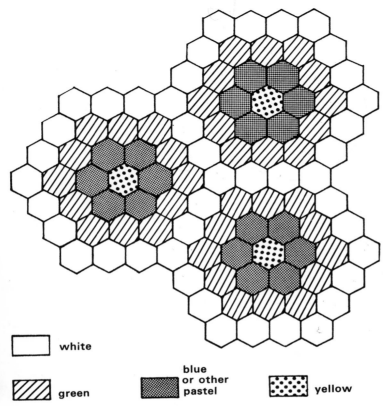

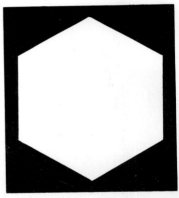

Illus. 39. Pattern for Grand-mother's Flower Garden Quilt. The traditional colors are as labelled.

Illus. 40. Pattern of the hexagon.

▢ white

▨ green

▨ blue or other pastel

▨ yellow

You make the entire quilt cover of small hexagons, six-sided patches, sewn together to resemble flowers. If you wish to make the quilt a true flower garden, cut the center hexagon of each block from yellow material, the next row from pink, blue, or another pastel material, the third row (the foliage row) from green and the connecting row from white. It is extremely important that you cut all pieces accurately so that all the edges are sharp.

To figure the amount of material you need for each color, decide how large you want the finished quilt to be; then, measure the hexagon and see how many will fit into $\frac{1}{2}$ yard of material. Estimate how many hexagons you need for the entire quilt and divide this total by the number you need of each color.

When you have cut the hexagons, select the middle hexagon and sew the second row to this middle piece, making a $\frac{1}{4}$-inch seam all round.

Next, sew the hexagons together with the same size seams. Continue adding row by row, sewing first the edges of the preceding row and then sewing the new row together. When you are ready to sew the path row or white row together, you have to join the flower blocks. See Illus. 39. Be sure that all the seams are straight and even.

When you have finished piecing this quilt, it will have a naturally scalloped border. Instead of turning the edge under and hemming it, sew bias tape round the edge to finish it off. If you only want the ends of the quilt scalloped, or only the edges, follow Illus. 42. Only piece part of the flower pattern, as shown in Illus. 42, instead of the full flower along the edges you want to be even. When you have completed this piecing, the edges of the quilt have small points, as shown. Cut these points off following the dotted line in Illus. 42. Then, finish the edge with bias tape or quilt binding.

To quilt, follow the seam lines around each hexagon, as shown in Illus. 41. Do not quilt through the middle of any patch.

This quilt is often made as a coverlet or bedspread with a dust ruffle added in a matching color.

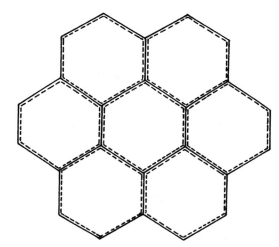

Illus. 41 (above). Suggested quilting lines for Grandmother's Flower Garden Quilt.

Illus. 42 (below). To scallop the edges, only piece part of the outside flower section as shown.

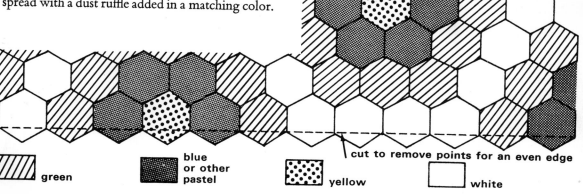

cut to remove points for an even edge

///// green

blue or other pastel

::::: yellow

☐ white

Illus. 43. This is a simple baby quilt appliquéd with randomly placed, multi-colored tulips.

Illus. 44. Fairy tales and nursery rhymes, such as Humpty Dumpty, are appropriate inspirations for children's quilts.

Appliquéd Quilts

Many beginning quilters shy away from appliqué patterns thinking they are too difficult or time consuming when quite the contrary is true. Appliqué quilts demand more skill in hand-sewing, but are often simpler and quicker to make than intricate patchwork. An appliquéd quilt is sometimes referred to as a "laid-on" quilt because you cut the pieces of the design out of different materials and lay them on or appliqué them to a plain background. You use a hemming stitch, slip stitch or buttonhole stitch to hold these pieces in place.

You must take great care when making an appliqué quilt to cut the pieces carefully and to allow $\frac{1}{4}$ inch on the pattern pieces for turning edges. As you cut the pieces, keep them in order by stringing them as you did for patchwork. Press all the pieces. Then, turn down the edges of each piece $\frac{1}{4}$ inch and crease them in place with your thumb and forefinger. If you do not turn under and stitch the pieces, they often pull out and the edges fray badly. You may have to make small cuts or notches $\frac{1}{8}$ inch deep in corners or sharp turns to maintain the outline of your pattern.

Baste these turned-down edges with a long run-making stitch. Since you will remove these basting threads, for identification use a contrasting thread color and keep your knot on the top of the piece. When you have turned and basted all the pieces, press them again with a warm iron. Now you are ready to assemble the over-all design you have chosen for each individual block or quilt top. Once you have set your pieces in place, hold them securely with a long basting stitch.

Appliqué Stitches

You can work the actual appliqué stitch in black embroidery thread, for an outline stitch, or a color to match the appliquéd piece for a less obvious stitch. Six-strand cotton embroidery floss works best for appliqué stitches, as you can use all six strands or less, if you separate the threads.

Just as your pattern design determines the quilting stitch you use, so it determines the appliqué stitch you use. Use the hemming stitch or slip stitch (Illus. 46) when you are sewing flowers or other delicate pattern pieces to the quilt top. Use the buttonhole stitch (Illus. 47), probably the most common appliqué stitch, to emphasize a particular part of a design or when each block contains one figure or motif, such as the tulip (see page 38) or sunbonnet girl (see page 40).

Illus. 45. This is the traditional bridal quilt pattern. Notice the lovely simplicity produced by hearts and leaves.

35

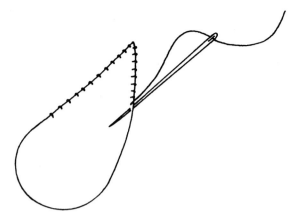

Illus. 46. Use the slip stitch for appliqué work in which you do not need to emphasize the outline of the design.

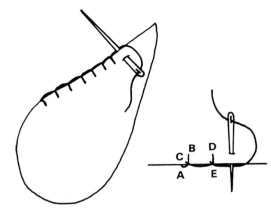

Illus. 47. Use the buttonhole stitch to emphasi a particular appliqué pattern piece. Follow t steps in the drawing on the right.

This buttonhole stitch not only produces a bold outline for appliqué pattern pieces that you want to emphasize, but it also holds the piece securely. It will not hold the edges, however, unless the stitches are close to each other. For this reason, when you use the buttonhole stitch, use a fine running stitch round the edges of the pattern piece to hold turned edges under and then do the buttonhole stitch over this. This way, when you pull the basting threads out, the material edges will not come out too. To make the buttonhole stitch, begin at the left and sew towards the right, looping the thread below the needle on each stitch (see Illus. 47). Finish thread strands off with a backstitch and a fine knot on the back of the appliqué piece.

Another appliqué stitch is a simple slip stitch for which you alternate long and short stitche making a decorative and fine, delicate stitch. T make this stitch, bring the needle out on the insid edge of the pattern piece, go in on the backgroun block, and come out again on the inside edge the pattern piece (see Illus. 48).

Use an appliqué stitch much like the hemmir stitch for work that does not require an outlin emphasis. Sewing right to left, catch the folde edge of the appliqué piece to the backgroun material. Take stitches less than $\frac{1}{8}$ inch long, the thread on the top of the pattern piece sho as little as possible.

Many of the new model sewing machines a equipped to do various outline or zig-zag stitche several of which are suited for machine appliqu work. The machine zig-zag or satin stitch mak

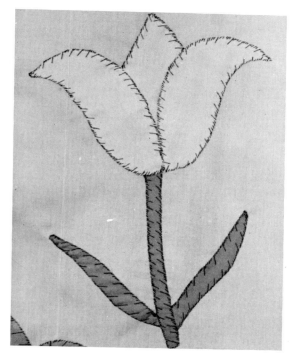

a neat appliqué outline and holds an appliqué design better than a loose hand stitch. In fact, if you work the machine stitches close to each other, depending on the material, you may not have to turn the edges on the appliqué pieces. If the material seems to have a tendency to fray, however, it is better to turn the edges. If you choose to

machine-stitch your design, experiment with the correct stitch length and width and the proper tension for your machine before beginning your actual quilt.

As with the patchwork quilt, if you are a beginning quilter, you would be wise to choose a simple pattern for your first appliqué quilt and then proceed to patterns with more intricate parts.

Illus. 49. The appliqué on this bridal quilt consists of machine-sewn zig-zag stitches.

Tulip Quilt

The Tulip Quilt is one of many quilts with flower patterns and this particular tulip is one of many tulip variations. This quilt is versatile and easy to piece for anyone regardless of past quilting experience. Because you frame each tulip in its own block, you can use any color combinations and the quilt can be either a spring-time color assortment or a one-color garden.

The recommended size for blocks for this quilt is approximately 14 × 16 inches which allows more room for the height of the flowers and

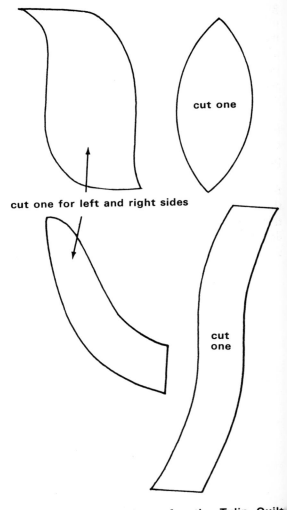

cut one

cut one for left and right sides

cut
one

Illus. 51. Pattern pieces for the Tulip Quilt

Illus. 50. An intricate motif is not necessary for an attractive quilt. These stylish but simple tulips are easy to piece.

gives each flower a block large enough to show it off. Usually, the tulips are pieced from solid material—any color for the flower and some shade of green for the stem and leaves. Cut all pattern pieces, according to the pattern in Illus. 51, from whatever colors you have chosen and turn the edges as directed on page 34.

Baste, then appliqué all flowers to the blocks (see Illus. 52). Set the quilt together with strips of material chosen to match either the flower petals or the green in the leaves.

Quilt this pattern around the edges of each flower petal and around the stem and leaves. If there is a blank space more than 3 inches within the flower block, quilt a small flower or other design in each corner so that the filling will not shift or bunch when you launder the quilt.

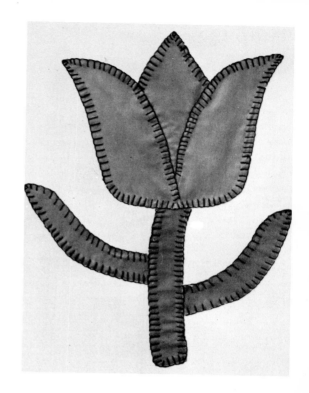

Illus. 52. Close-up of the appliqué stitches on the tulip.

Sunbonnet Sue
and Overall Sam

Sunbonnet Sue (see Illus. 55) and her friend Overall Sam (see Illus. 37) can be found in many different poses on quilt tops everywhere. These two charming figures seem to be most popular for grandmothers to make for their grandchildren. Many little girls have a Sunbonnet Sue dressed in

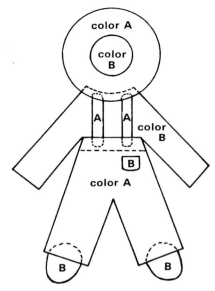

Illus. 54. Pattern for Overall Sam.

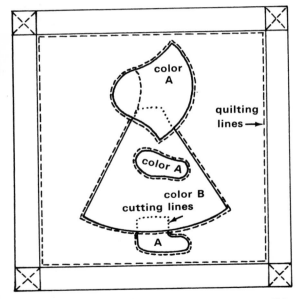

Illus. 53. Cut Sunbonnet Sue along the solid lines, following the dotted lines for the shoes and bodice top. You may follow the straight broken lines for quilting.

all the same dresses she has. What a nice way for a little girl to remember her childhood days.

For these patterns, appliqué either the boy or girl figure or both onto a white background block. Use small prints for the dresses and shirts and solids for the pants and hats.

Overall Sam is simple to make and you can sew him as elaborately or as simply as you desire. Although in Illus. 37, Sam is not wearing blue denim overalls, he can be a real farm hand with blue denim overalls and a sun hat. If you cannot get soft blue denim, use brown, navy blue, or any dark-colored cotton you wish. Often, Sam is combined in a quilt with Sunbonnet Sue and his shirt is made from the same material as her dress.

Blocks for this quilt can be as large as 15 inches square or as small as 8 inches square. Simply draw your pattern figure to fit whichever size block you use, leaving some border space within the block on all sides. See Illus. 53 and 54 for the patterns. Cut all pattern pieces, prepare and baste them according to the directions in the appliqué section on page 34. Make sure you cut Sam's suspenders (braces) long enough to tuck under his hat and pants.

Stitch all pieces onto the blocks. When you have appliquéd all the blocks, you can set the quilt together. At this time, if you wish to personalize the quilt, you can put balloons in the girl's hand or embroider flowers round the band of her hat. Add a pocket to Sam's pants, if you want, or, to make him an authentic farm boy, place a small, cloth triangle handkerchief inside the pocket of his shirt. For a real blue-jean look, you can top-stitch with white thread round the edges of his pants. Additional embroidery you can add to Sam's block includes a fishing pole and bucket, a dog or cat, or a hoe and shovel.

Quilt Sunbonnet Sue around the edge of the figure and around her arm and the entire hat (see Illus. 53). Quilt Sam, like Sue, around the outline of the figure and then around the hat, inside rim and center circle, then along the suspenders and pants top.

If you make larger figures, quilt through the band of both hats and across the top of Sam's pants.

Illus. 55. Close-up of Sunbonnet Sue. Add flowers, if you wish, for an individual touch.

Illus. 56. Close-up of Overall Sam. Notice the machine-sewn zig-zag appliqué stitches.

41

Rose Quilt

Like the Tulip, the Rose Quilt has many pattern variations. Most patterns following this basic design are referred to as Rose of Sharon quilts. Color selections and border designs seem to determine whether or not the quilt is called Rose of Sharon. The woman who made the quilt described here simply calls hers the Rose Quilt.

This pattern consists of one large flower with a smaller center surrounded by four buds or flowers and a circle of foliage. The quilt looks quite nice as a two-color pattern, using light and dark shades of the same color for the flower and buds, and green for the stems and leaves. You can set the quilt together with one of the flower colors.

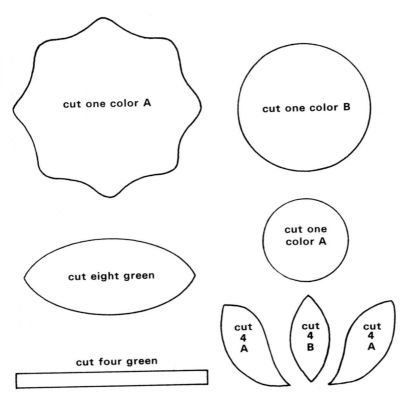

cut one color A

cut one color B

cut eight green

cut one color A

Illus. 57. Pattern pieces for the Rose Quilt. The actual size you cut the roses depends on the size you want the finished quilt to be.

cut four green

cut 4 A

cut 4 B

cut 4 A

Illus. 58. Suggested quilting pattern for the Rose Quilt.

Blocks for this quilt can be from 15 to 20 inches square. If you would like a different effect, appliqué the flower arrangement directly onto a solid quilt top eliminating the use of blocks.

Cut all necessary pattern pieces in the colors you have selected (see Illus. 57), turn the edges under and baste. Place the cut-out pieces on the quilt block and slip the stems under the large flower and under the smaller buds so the ends do not show. When you have placed all the stems, baste the pieces down and appliqué the flowers in place. Sew the leaves on the quilt last, so that you can center them between the extended buds.

When you have completed the blocks, piece them with strips and set the quilt together. Quilting directions for this quilt are like those for most appliqué quilts: follow the lines of the pattern and quilt around each separate pattern piece (see Illus. 58). A border is not called for in this pattern and is, therefore, optional. However, if you do choose to put a large border on the quilt, consider decorating it with the same flower you placed in the center of the block. Such a border is often added to this quilt.

Illus. 36 shows this Rose Quilt in color.

Baby Quilts

Baby quilts are something special. They seem to carry more love in each piece than any quilt four times their size, and what a lovely addition to any newborn's layette! Baby quilts, because of their size, are so simple to make that every baby might have one made by a mother, grandmother or family friend.

If you have been hesitant to begin a full-sized quilt, what better way to try a pattern than in miniature? Infant quilts offer an excellent opportunity for the quilter anxious to design a new pattern to start on a small scale. You can make baby quilts from any pattern you like, but there are a few patterns especially suitable for infant quilts. Animals, small block designs, nursery-rhyme figures and pastel flower bouquets are popular motifs for baby quilts.

You must be more selective than usual in choosing material for a baby quilt, however. Remember that even though most quilts will not be next to or touch the baby's skin, the fabric should be soft and easily washable, just in case. Always pre-wash material for an infant quilt to remove excessive dyes and soften the material.

When choosing a filling for your baby quilt, keep in mind that you will probably launder the quilt frequently. The new dacron (terylene) and polyester fillings are light and fluffy and launder beautifully.

Baby quilts may vary in size from 36 × 36 to 45 inches square or larger. The size of the quilt depends on the pattern you select and on the type of quilt you are making. A throw quilt need not be as large as a quilt to be used for a crib blanket, and a quilt or coverlet designed for a cradle or carriage can be smaller than a crib quilt.

Infant quilts are easy to machine-quilt because of their small size. Also, some need not be put into a frame to be quilted, and you can simply baste them securely around the edges and through the middle with a large X.

Although you usually hem quilts with an overlap of the backing material, infant quilts seem to have more of a finished look when you place binding round the edges. Binding is inexpensive and easy to use. Follow the directions on the binding package or the steps in Illus. 8 to 10 on pages 13 to 14.

Teddy Bear Quilt

This Teddy Bear Quilt was designed by the author as her little girl's first quilt. It makes a wonderful homecoming present for any new mother and baby. The center square (see Illus. 59) is reserved for the baby's name, birth date, and any other special information you might want to add. Because the bear figures are one simple

Illus. 60. Pattern for the teddy bear.

Illus. 59. Reserve the middle square for the baby's name and birthdate or any other embroidery or appliqué you want.

pattern (see Illus. 60), this quilt is easy and fun to make.

Since the size of the quilt depends on how you plan to use it, specific size requirements are not given, just general directions for assembly and quilting. In the pictured quilt, the bears are appliquéd onto individual blocks, then set together with strips of material with small connecting blocks. The strips match the material chosen for the quilt back. You could, however, place the bears on one solid piece of material and leave an open space in the middle of the quilt to embroider the child's name.

After you have attached the bears to the blocks, using a hand appliqué or machine zig-zag stitch,

45

Illus. 61. Close-up of the teddy bear. Note the touch the embroidered butterfly adds.

Humpty Dumpty Quilt

The Humpty Dumpty Quilt, designed from the famous nursery story of the same name, makes a decorative quilt or a charming wall hanging for a child's room. The figures on the quilt are large and bold and take up most of the quilt top space, so there is no need for an elaborate design.

The quilt in Illus. 44 was made from fuzzy cotton knit pieces, sewn to the quilt top with a zig-zag appliqué stitch. The smaller background pieces (the bricks) were placed on first, then Humpty Dumpty was set on the brick wall. You can sew additional figures to the quilt pattern and you can scale the quilt to any desired size. Although this quilt was machine appliquéd, it was hand-quilted around Humpty Dumpty and the smaller pieces. The remainder of the quilt was quilted in straight lines, approximately 2 inches apart, from top to bottom.

Humpty Dumpty is just one example of making a quilt from a popular children's story or poem. Children identify with and remember the story that goes with them. Do not forget all the quilting possibilities in other popular nursery rhymes and story books.

embroider eyes, nose, mouth and paws. You can embroider the information about the child at this time or after you have assembled the quilt. Because this pattern is so simple, embroidery changes the appearance of each quilt. You can embroider delicate flowers, birds or any other design to give your quilt a very personal touch.

Quilt around the outside edge of each bear, and along the seam lines of the separating strips. Small quilted flowers or a scroll design will fill the center block very well.

Teddy bears seem to be popular with children of all ages. To enlarge this quilt for use by an older child, either make larger teddy bears or simply cut more of them.

Tacked Quilts

Tacked or tied quilts are just what their name implies. Instead of using quilting stitches to hold the three quilt layers together, you tie yarn or crochet thread in double knots, at intervals, through all three layers, as was done in early colonial quilts. Tacked quilts are just as sturdy as quilted ones, and much faster to make, but you must space the knots or tacked points fairly close together.

Most tacked quilts are square patch quilts with knots tied in the corners and in the middle of each block. You can adapt almost any pattern to a tacked design, if you work out an attractive pattern for tying the knots.

To tack your quilt, thread a large-eyed needle with heavy crochet thread or knitting worsted. Using the thread double, push the needle from the top through all three quilt layers, leaving the thread end on top. Push the needle up from the bottom of the quilt about $\frac{1}{2}$ inch away from the first thread. Tie the thread in a firm double knot and clip the ends of the thread, leaving at least $\frac{1}{2}$ inch.

You can use cotton or dacron (terylene) filling

Illus. 62. Instead of quilting, you may tack a quilt by tying knots either in the corners and middle of your patched squares, as shown here, or in any decorative pattern you design.

in tacked quilts. Many quilters use new light-weight acrylic blankets between the quilt layers for an extra heavy quilt, or a sheet for a light-weight quilt. You can use heavier materials for making tacked quilts than those you use for quilted ones. Many beautiful tacked quilts are even made from wool pieces. There certainly could be no warmer blanket on a cold winter night.

If you enjoy patchwork, piece a quilt and invite your friends to a tacking party. There is no need to put a tacked quilt in a frame, if you baste it securely, and then anyone can come and help you tie a few knots here and there.

Design Your Own Quilts

When our great-grandmothers made quilts, they relied on their own imaginations for quilt designs, and everything around them became a potential pattern. Trees and leaves, a garden trellis, a water pump, flowers, and garden plants inspired the patterns still used in quilting today. Too often, however, quilters rely entirely on standard patterns and are at a loss for making their own designs.

Even if you have an urge to create an individual pattern, you may not know where to begin. You start drawing in some hodge-podge fashion and end up nowhere. Before you become discouraged, take a hint from earlier quilters—often the simplest natural things make the most beautiful patterns. Look closely at flowers or leaves, find the design in a seashell, see how honeysuckle vines climb, look at birds silhouetted against the sky. If you live in the city, look at windows in a large office building, find a pattern in buildings lining the street, catch a glimpse of a large bridge from a new angle, or look at the pattern streets make on a city map.

There is, in addition, a new trend in quilt-making. Quilters today are not making quilts out of necessity for warmth, but rather as a means of self expression and as a chance to make something with their hands. With this new interest in quilting, quilts are no longer confined to use as bedcovers. Now, they decorate walls, floors and furniture, and, with a slight sizing variation, appear at parties as women's skirts and capes. Needless to say, with these new uses for quilts, come new and bolder designs. Quilts are covered with faces taken from photographs, full-sized bodies reclining, and abstract figures running and dancing. New symbols of the times are popular themes for quilts—the ecology movements, the peace dove and space flights.

This trend of using the quilt as a means of art expression is not really new, although early quilters may not have been aware of the masterpieces they were creating. While some quilters just did what came natural and followed their eye for color, they created some thoroughly modern geometric patterns on their quilt tops which are now hanging in craft museums. Quilting is not new and certainly beautiful patterns are not new. There are just a lot of people discovering the world of quilting for the first time.

Simply making a quilt is a very rewarding thing —you will have a special pride in seeing your own handiwork, especially in something people will use. You can feel even more satisfied when the quilt is your own unique design. After you know the basics of putting a quilt together, experiment with new and different designs. Let the next quilt you make really be a part of you.

TRAPUNTO

decorative quilting

Before You Begin Trapuntoing

Trapunto, sometimes called Italian quilting, is a form of quilting in which you raise only a specially chosen design. You stitch along this design through two layers of fabric and then insert stuffing between the two layers. You may either hand stitch or machine stitch the design with matching or contrasting thread or yarn. Add Trapunto to an article of clothing or household item that you have purchased or incorporate it into an item that you make yourself.

In either case, you need crisp *woven* "interfacing" (available in fabric and sewing shops) for the backing fabric. If you use a lighter weight fabric than interfacing, the raised effect, which results from stuffing, shows more on the wrong side than on the right side. With interfacing for a backing, however, you force the raised design to the right side. If you choose to stitch your design by hand, you must first decide how prominent you wish your stitching to be before you choose between yarn, embroidery floss (soft cotton thread for embroidery), or sewing thread in a matching or contrasting color. You may use regular sewing thread and straight machine stitching unless you wish the stitching to show. In that case, use special buttonhole twist thread.

The method you use for stuffing depends on your design. You can get some idea of the different methods by following the instructions for the various projects in this book. Generally, use polyester fibre (called 100 per cent polyester fibre), which you can buy in fabric and sewing shops, for stuffing all areas other than narrow strips, such as flower stems or stripes. For such narrow areas, use yarn or cording as stuffing.

General Items for Your Home

Take a critical tour of your home. Every room, you will find, contains potential Trapunto material, since the Trapunto technique readily lends itself to the decoration of many different items.

Initial Pillow

Begin in your living room or den. If your couch or armchair needs an extra something, try personalizing a solid color, cotton suede pillow like the one in Illus. 1. To make an initial pillow, sketch the letter you choose on a piece of paper. When the shape of the letter suits you, draw another set of lines beside the first ones, exactly $\frac{1}{4}''$ away. Use a ruler, measuring at frequent intervals, to be sure of the $\frac{1}{4}''$-spacing. Draw a decorative border round the initials for the edges of the pillow. You may draw a straight border, like the one in Illus. 63, or be creative and make up an interesting one of your own. Again, each pair of lines should be $\frac{1}{4}''$ apart.

When you finish your design, re-trace the lines with a black felt-tip pen. Turn the paper over and trace the design on the wrong side of the paper. Use this wrong side in the next step. Cut a piece of crisp woven interfacing the size you want your finished pillow to be, plus $\frac{5}{8}''$ seam allowances on all sides. Place the interfacing over the wrong side of the design. You must use the wrong side of the design or your letter will be backwards on the

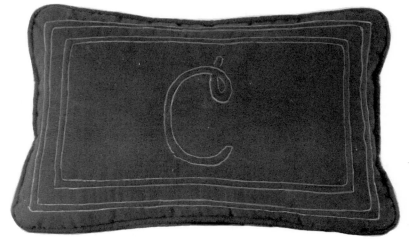

Illus. 63. An initial pillow is a simple, yet attractive, first Trapunto project. Avoid backtacking (back stitching) and broken threads, as are shown here, as they will spoil your creation.

finished pillow. Using a sharp, soft lead pencil, trace the backwards design onto the interfacing.

Cut a piece of fabric for your pillow front the same size as the interfacing. Place the two pieces—fabric and interfacing—together with the right side of the pillow face down on a table. Put the interfacing on top of the fabric, making sure that the side with the pencilled drawing faces up. (The

letter should look backwards.) Carefully pin these two pieces of fabric together. If you wish, you may baste them together, since it is very important that they do not slip.

Fill your sewing machine bobbin with button hole twist in a color that contrasts with the pillow fabric. Use regular thread of the same color on top of the machine. On a scrap of fabric, test your machine's tension. It must be properly adjusted because the bobbin thread appears on the right side of the pillow cover. If the tension is off, follow the directions in the booklet that accompanies your machine to correct it. (If you wish to stitch this by hand, follow the directions on page 62.)

With the interfacing facing you, stitch along all the lines you have drawn, using a long stitch (six stitches per inch). Never cross a line of stitching to finish off. Instead, stop, tie the ends on the wrong side, and then begin stitching again on the other side. *Never* backtack (back stitch) when machine stitching. You must pull the threads to the wrong side and tie them, because backtacking always shows and looks sloppy. In Illus. 63, you can see where backtacking has spoiled the otherwise professional look of the pillow.

After you have finished stitching, thread a blunt-end, size 18 tapestry needle with yarn or cording. Poke a hole in the interfacing with the needle, taking care not to break the threads of the fabric or interfacing. Carefully work the threaded needle through the stitched area. Turn the corners and curves by bringing the needle out of the interfacing, then by re-inserting it, leaving a small loop of yarn, as shown in Illus. 64. You must leave this loop so that when the pillow, or any other

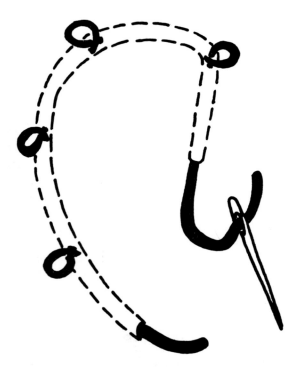

Illus. 64. In turning corners and curves in yarn-stuffed Trapunto you must leave a small loop of yarn as shown here.

project you make, is cleaned, there is some slack to allow for any possible shrinkage of the yarn. Trim the yarn at the beginning and the end, close to the fabric. Tug gently on the fabric so that the ends of the yarn slip into the holes and lie entirely between the two layers of fabric. With the point of the needle, coax the threads of the interfacing around the hole you poked with the needle back together. Repeat this process as often as necessary to completely fill the area between the stitches.

Cut another piece of fabric for the back of your pillow the same size as the front, either of the same fabric or of a matching or contrasting one. You can make cording from scraps of fabric and sew it to the right side of the pillow or make tassels from yarn for further decoration. With the right sides of the fabric together, stitch three sides and all four corners of the pillow (see Illus. 65). Turn the pillow right side out, making sure that each corner is completely turned. Make an inner pillow, from any light- to medium-weight fabric, $\frac{1}{4}''$ larger on all sides than your Trapunto pillow cover. Stuff the inner pillow with a bought pillow form or with polyester stuffing. Hand sew the fourth side closed.

Rose Pillow

You can make a different type of Trapunto pillow if you vary the Trapunto technique by using an appliqué and embroidery.

The rose pillow in Illus. 79, for example, does not have the interfacing you used for the initial pillow. Instead, draw your design on paper. When you are sure the design is exactly as you want it, trace over the lines with a black felt-tip marker. Place the design under the fabric. Care-

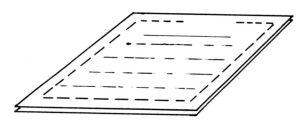

Illus. 65. To assemble a pillow, first place the right sides of the front and back together. Then stitch three sides and all four corners.

fully and lightly trace your design onto the right side of the fabric with fabric chalk.

Cut out a piece of another fabric to use as the appliqué, making sure that you leave an extra $\frac{1}{4}''$ for a hem to turn under. In this case, the rose bud is cut from red fabric. Trim the appliqué as necessary, then turn the hem under and press. Attach the appliqué to the fabric with a blind stitch—that is, take very tiny stitches on the bottom side of the appliqué and attach it with very tiny stitches to the pillow itself. Leave a small opening when you stitch, through which you stuff the appliqué with polyester fibre. Push the polyester fibre in with a quickpoint needle (blunt-end, size 13 tapestry needle). Close the hole, again with tiny blind stitches. You can make appliqués for the stem and leaves, or you can embroider them, following the markings from your original design.

Assemble this pillow according to the directions above. If you wish, you may insert lace into the seam before you sew it, as in Illus. 79.

Afghan

An afghan is a luxurious article with which to decorate any room. Make an afghan like the one pictured in Illus. 18 from a 60″ square, double thickness of polyester double knit fabric. Sew an original design (Illus. 66) in opposite corners—or, if you wish, in all four corners. In either case, first trace the design onto the interfacing according to the directions on page 53. The interfacing only has to be an inch or two larger than the actual drawn design, because the design only covers a

small portion of the afghan, unlike the initial pillow on page 53, where the design is over-all.

Very carefully place the interfacing in the corners of one layer of the wrong side of the fabric. Baste or pin the interfacing in position. Again, remember to check the tension on your machine, because the bobbin thread appears on the right side of your afghan. Using regular thread in a matching color, stitch along the drawn design leaving a 1″ opening (see Illus. 67).

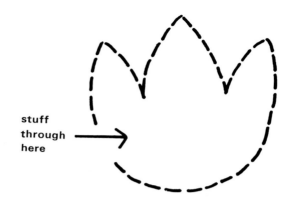

stuff through here →

Pull the threads to the back and tie. If you wish to stitch this design by hand, follow the instructions on page 62. Stuff the chosen areas with polyester fibre. Use a knitting needle to push the polyester to the ends of each section you are stuffing. Since the double knit fabric stretches easily, you may tend to overstuff. *Do not overstuff.* Remember that your design only needs to be slightly raised to be effective Trapunto. The more you stuff the

Illus. 68. Close-up of the afghan after it was stuffed.

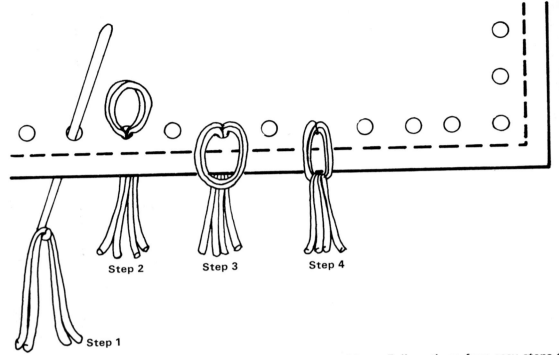

Step 1

Step 2

Step 3

Step 4

Illus. 69. With a pencil, make dots where you want to place fringe. Follow these four easy steps to attach the fringe.

design, the more likely puckering is to occur. You cannot avoid a certain amount of puckering, which varies with the kind of fabric that you use. The more "give" the fabric has, the less puckering there will be. Sew up the 1″ opening.

When you have finished stuffing your design, place another piece of the double knit fabric (the same size—60″ × 60″) on top of the one with the Trapunto design, right sides together. Stitch, ½″

from the edge on three sides and round all four corners, as you did for the pillows (Illus. 65). Turn the afghan right side out and stitch the fourth side by hand. Top stitch all the way round the afghan ½″ from the edge. This keeps the two pieces of fabric in place.

Use yarn of a matching or contrasting color for the fringe. Six ounces of yarn makes enough knotted fringe for a 60″ × 60″ afghan. Cut about

480 strands, each 20″ long. With a pencil, place dots 1″ apart just over the top stitching on the right side of the afghan. Using a large-sized crochet hook, poke a hole through both thicknesses of the afghan (see Illus. 69). Hook two strands of yarn (in the middle of each strand) onto the hook (Step 1) and pull through, so that about a 2″-loop appears on the right side of the afghan

(Step 2). Pull the ends of the yarn strands through the loop (Step 3). Pull tightly, but not so much that the fabric wrinkles (Step 4). Put three 2″-strand pieces in each corner hole. Follow Illus. 70 for knotting instructions for decorative fringe.

If you use a synthetic yarn (rather than wool), your afghan will be completely machine washable and dryable.

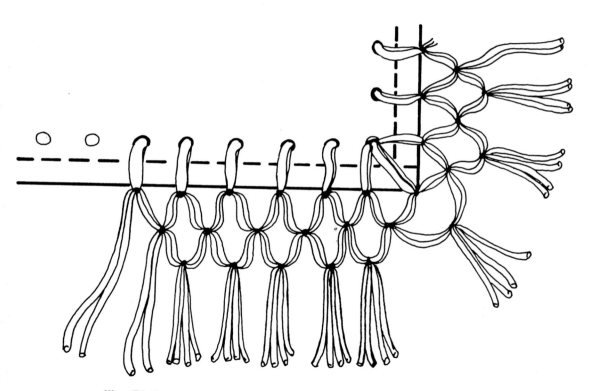

Illus. 70. For a more decorative fringe, follow this knotting pattern.

Table-Top Catch-All

Anyone who does any kind of handiwork is perpetually plagued by small piles of yarn, thread, fabric scraps and other trash. A table-top catch-all like the burlap-covered one in Illus. 74 is the perfect answer to help keep your den or sewing room tidy. Decorate a one-pound tin coffee can with Trapunto.

Burlap is easy to work with and fits into a casual or modern décor, but you can, of course, use any fabric you like. Cut whatever fabric you choose so that it goes round the tin can with a 1″ lap—that is, leave 1″ extra on one end. (Cut one end on the selvage, if possible.) Allow an extra 1½″ to fold under the bottom of the can. Also, allow an extra 3″ to fold into the top of the can (see Illus. 71).

Draw your design on a piece of paper the same size as the fabric, being sure to mark just where the hems are. You may draw one single motif, an over-all motif, or a border design at the top and bottom. You certainly do not need to be an established artist to create an effective design. There are many subjects that you can even trace. Children's coloring books, appliqué books, and learn-to-draw art books all have simple, bold designs. You can also use magazine pictures as a guide for sketching a freehand design. Furthermore, you may enlarge or reduce any design by using the grid method.

To enlarge a design, for example, draw a $\frac{1}{4}$″-grid, which is simply a series of criss-crossed lines $\frac{1}{4}$″ apart (see Illus. 72), over the design to be

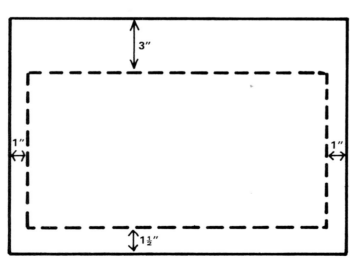

Illus. 71. Cut fabric for a table-top catch-all with these extra allowances on the edges.

Illus. 72. Draw a $\frac{1}{4}$-inch grid over the original design you wish to enlarge.

Illus. 74. Trapunto projects can be practical as well as attractive. A table-top catch-all has innumerable uses.

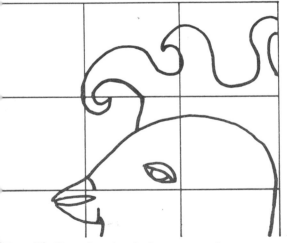

Illus. 73. Transfer the design square by square onto a 1-inch grid, thus increasing the design four times.

enlarged. On another piece of paper, draw a $1''$-grid—criss-crossed lines $1''$ apart—using the same number of squares as the $\frac{1}{4}''$-grid. Sketching freehand, copy the lines within each of the small squares of the $\frac{1}{4}''$-grid to each of the squares of the $1''$-grid (see Illus. 73). The $\frac{1}{4}''$- and $1''$-grids increase the original design four times. By varying the size of the grids, you can vary the final size of your design. Reverse the size of the grids—that is, draw a $1''$-grid over the original design and transfer the lines to a $\frac{1}{4}''$-grid—to reduce the design to one quarter the original size.

Now, transfer your design to the interfacing, which should be the same size as the burlap, as described on page 53. Be sure that your design is well-centered on the burlap. Pin the interfacing securely to the burlap.

Burlap's ruggedness demands rugged stitching. Large stitches, hand-sewn with yarn, give this desired look (see Illus. 75). Take $\frac{1}{4}''$ running

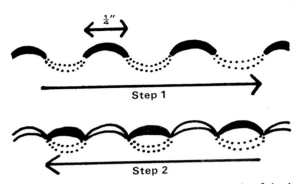

Illus. 76. To hand stitch a design, take $\frac{1}{4}$-inch running stitches. Repeat, going under where you went over and vice versa. The dotted lines show the stitches on the wrong side of the fabric.

stitches, leaving a $\frac{1}{2}''$- to $\frac{3}{4}''$-opening somewhere between the stitches. Next, go back over the stitches you just made, this time going under where you went over and vice versa (see Illus. 76). This makes the line of stitching so secure that the stuffing cannot ooze out. Stuff each section of your design and then close up the opening with the same stitching before going on to the next section.

When you have finished, cover the tin can by wrapping the fabric round it as tightly as you can. Pin the lapped ends in place so that the selvage end is on top; this eliminates excessive bulk. Blind stitch the two ends together as described on page 55. Fold under the excess fabric at the bottom and tape it to the tin can with masking tape. Repeat the process at the top, and your catch-all is ready for use. Start immediately by putting in it the left-over yarn scraps, burlap and masking tape.

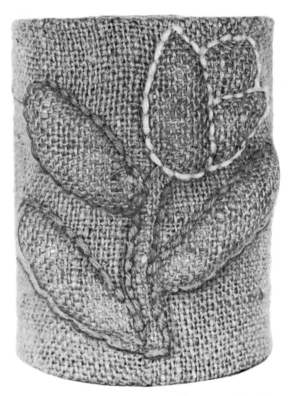

Illus. 75. Close-up of the table-top catch-all.

Illus. 77. Close-up of the eagle picture on page 64.

Eagle Picture

Now that you have made Trapunto to enliven your furniture, to keep you cosy in winter and to store your odds and ends in, why not also make Trapunto to hang on your wall? Make an eagle like the one in Illus. 78 or choose your own design. For a different Trapunto effect, outline the eagle with a double line of stitching and stuff that rather than stuff whole areas (see Illus. 77). Choose a simple design and draw it in parallel lines $\frac{1}{4}''$ apart on a piece of paper. Using a ruler, measure at frequent intervals to be sure that your lines are $\frac{1}{4}''$ apart. Transfer the final design to a piece of interfacing as described on page 53.

For the pictures, choose an outer fabric that complements your décor. Cut it so that there is at least $1\frac{1}{2}''$-margin on all sides. Use buttonhole twist thread in your bobbin and use regular thread of the same color on top of the machine. Again, check your tension, as the bobbin thread shows on the right side of your picture. Stitch (six stitches per inch) on all lines. Be very careful to follow your lines. Never cross one line of stitching

Illus. 78. Make a Trapunto creation to frame and hang up. Notice that only thin areas between double lines of stitching were stuffed.

with another and do not backtack. Pull all threads to the wrong side and tie. As usual, you may stitch the design by hand. See page 62 for instructions.

After stitching, stuff between the lines with yarn threaded on a blunt-end tapestry needle. Follow the instructions on page 54.

To frame your picture, you must first mount it on a piece of thin plywood or Masonite (pressed board). Cut the board so that it fits into your frame, making sure to allow for the thickness of the fabric. Center the design over the Masonite; fold under the excess fabric and tape it in place. Trim the corners to eliminate bulk, but be careful. If you trim too much, the fabric may ravel. Insert the board and the attached picture into the frame and hang your picture proudly.

Illus. 79. An interesting Trapunto technique is to use an appliqué—such as the rose bud here—and to stuff that rather than the entire design.

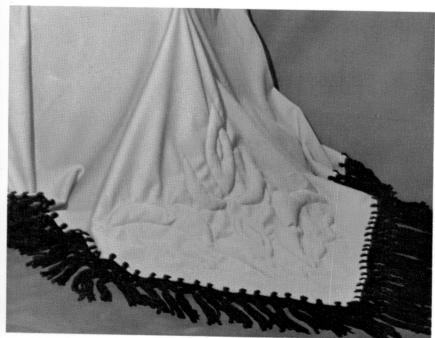

Illus. 80. An afghan adds special warmth to any room. Decorate one corner or all four with an original Trapunto design.

Fruit Picture

Decorate your dining room walls with a unusual still life. Prepare your picture (Illus. 81) o felt, an excellent material for Trapunto, the sam way as you did the eagle on page 63. For variet and interest, however, you can change sever artistic aspects. If you use thread that matches th fabric, rather than a complementary thread, th stitching lines and the Trapunto design stand ou quite noticeably, relying entirely on your Trapunt for emphasis.

Illus. 82 (left). Tired of that bowl of fruit on your table? Make a truly unique still life with Trapunto.

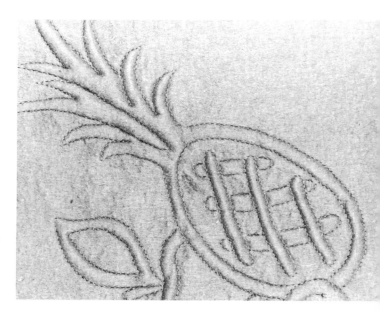

Illus. 81. Close-up of the fruit picture.

Accessories for
Your Kitchen

Toaster and Mixer Covers

Co-ordinated kitchen appliance covers decorated with Trapunto are sanitary and useful as well as attractive. Neither the colors nor the designs have to match. In fact, complementary colors, as were used for the toaster and mixer covers in Illus. 86, add a special creative effect to your kitchen.

Terry cloth, used for these appliance covers, is another fabric which lends itself well to Trapunto. Note in Illus. 83 and 84, how little puckering there is. Like burlap, terry cloth has a rugged quality and, therefore, you should hand stitch your design with yarn.

Put your design onto the interfacing by the same process described on page 53. If you choose to make covers from a commercial pattern, do the Trapunto before you sew any seams. Stuff with polyester fibre as directed on page 57. Then, assemble the covers according to the pattern directions. If you want to put the design on a purchased cover, buy one of a solid color and use your own design on it.

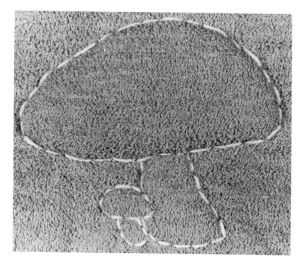

Illus. 83 (above). Design stitched and stuffed on the toaster cover.

Illus. 84 (below). Design stitched and stuffed on the mixer cover.

You may also choose a printed cover and stuff all or part of the design already on it (see page 63). In this case, work from the right side of the fabric. Stitch along the design on the machine using thread whose color will show the least. This is because the printed design—not the stitching—is of primary interest. Follow the stitching instructions on page 54 and then stuff according to the directions on page 57.

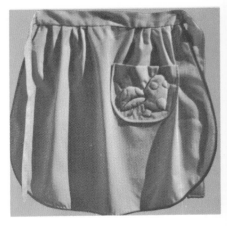

Illus. 85. Serve a delicious home-made dinner in this handsome apron decorated with Trapunto.

Illus. 86. Keep your kitchen appliances shiny and dust-free with easy-to-make Trapunto covers.

68

Apron

Add a decorative or even glamorous touch to an apron that you have made or have bought. If the apron already has a pocket on it, like the apron on the front cover and in Illus. 85, carefully remove the pocket, put your Trapunto design on it, and then sew the pocket back onto the apron. If your apron does not have a pocket, use a contrasting piece of solid-colored fabric to make one. If you are making your own apron, put the Trapunto design on the pocket before you sew the pocket on the apron.

Transfer a design onto a piece of interfacing that is the same size as the pocket, following the directions on page 53.

Stitch, using a contrasting color, with buttonhole twist thread in the bobbin and the same color regular thread on top of the machine. Ordinarily, it is not attractive for one line of stitching to cross another when you are going to stuff both areas. Note that the stem of the mushroom on the left in Illus. 97, however, is not stuffed. In some instances, therefore, stitching can cross other stitching. The tufts of grass in Illus. 87 are hand-embroidered with embroidery floss.

Be careful not to overstuff the apron design. Cotton and cotton blend fabrics especially do not have much "give" and overstuffing would cause excessive and unattractive puckering.

Illus. 87. Close-up of the apron's pocket design.

Pot Holders

Utilitarian items, such as the pot holders in Illus. 92, can also be colorful and imaginative. Choose designs appropriate for the kitchen—draw fruit or even continue the mushroom theme from the apron if you like. Trace your design onto a piece of interfacing the same size as the pot holder. The pot holders in Illus. 92 are made of poplin, which has little or no "give" and, therefore, results in excessive puckering, but any sturdy, washable fabric with a close weave is also suitable.

Stitch, using colored yarn, which emphasizes your design, according to the directions on page 62. Carefully plan your stitching so that you can stuff as you go.

Stuff with polyester fibre. You must stuff the small areas round the orange sections in Illus. 88

Illus. 89. Close-up of the red pot holder picture on page 72.

by poking a hole in the interfacing as described on page 54. For these small areas, use a blunt-end tapestry needle as described on page 55.

Embroider seeds, as in Illus. 88 and 89, in yarn on top of the pot holder after you finish the Trapunto.

To assemble your pot holder, cut a piece of fabric for the back which is the same size as the front piece. Place the right sides together and stitch three sides and all four corners (see page 55). Turn the pot holder right side out. Insert a piece of cotton batting (a special material made to use in quilts), which is slightly smaller than the pot holder, between the two layers. You could also make a good insulator from an old wash cloth or two. Stitch the fourth side by hand and your handy needlework is ready for use and display.

Illus. 88. Close-up of the orange pot holder pictured on page 72.

Children's Room

Rocking Chair Cushion

Spruce up an antique child's rocker (or a new one) with a Trapunto seat. Carefully sand and finish the wood, if necessary.

Choose a piece of printed fabric that a child would like and also one that will complement the décor of the child's room. Select a print that is neither too busy nor too detailed. The fabric could have three or four main areas of interest, as shown in Illus. 90, or just one main area for you to stuff, as in Illus. 91. The size and number of stuffed areas depend on the size of the project. A chair seat, for example, could have a larger design area than could a pot holder.

Measure the seat of the rocker. Cut four long, thin ($\frac{5}{8}''$) strips of paper and paste or staple them together to form a frame. Be sure that the *inside* measurement of the frame is the size you want your seat to be. Move the frame over the fabric.

Illus. 90. For a large item—such as a picture or a pillow—choose a print fabric with several areas of interest. Stuff, for example, the daisies, their stems and leaves, and the butterfly.

Illus. 91. For a smaller item— such as a pot holder—you could simply choose one section of a larger printed fabric to stuff.

cut on
this line

Illus. 93. With a paper frame, select the part of the pattern you like for a pillow for a rocking chair seat. Cut along the outside of the frame.

Select the portion of the fabric which will give the most pleasing and well-balanced seat cover (see Illus. 93). With a pencil, draw a line (or dots which you can connect later) round the *outside* of the paper frame on the fabric. This will be the size of the finished seat cover, including a $\frac{5}{8}''$ seam allowance. Cut the fabric on this line. Then, cut a piece of interfacing the same size, and attach it by pinning it or basting it to the fabric.

Choose the sections of the print that you would like to stuff. You may stuff all printed sections, if you like. Whichever you do, be sure to try for a well-balanced design.

Stitch either by hand or machine, but use a color thread that does not stand out. The printed fabric is of primary interest, not the stitching. Stitch.

Stuff the small areas of your design, by first poking a hole in the interfacing, being careful not to break the threads. Then, stuff with polyester fibre and push the interfacing threads back together. Stitch and stuff the large areas as you did the afghan (see pages 56–57).

Cut another piece of the same fabric for the back of the cushion, or use a piece of solid color fabric. Stitch as you did for the pillow (page 55). Insert a foam rubber seat cushion and hand stitch the fourth side. Spray the cushion with a water-proofing product.

If the rocker is an antique and has a cane bottom that needs replacing, you can still make a Trapunto seat. Cut your fabric bigger than you would for a cushion. After you have selected (using the

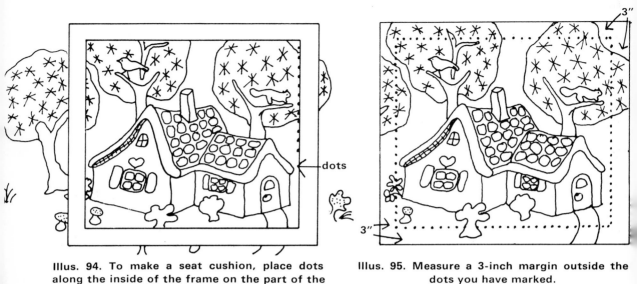

Illus. 94. To make a seat cushion, place dots along the inside of the frame on the part of the fabric you wish to use.

Illus. 95. Measure a 3-inch margin outside the dots you have marked.

paper frame) the area of fabric that will be your seat, place dots, very lightly, on the *inside* of the frame. Using a ruler, add a 3″ margin all the way round (see Illus. 94 and 95).

Stitch and stuff. Cut a piece of $\frac{1}{4}$″ plywood or a piece of Masonite (pressed board) $\frac{1}{8}$″ smaller than the finished size of your seat. Place the Trapunto over it. Fold under the edges and staple the Trapunto in place.

Spray the seat with a waterproofing product. Place it on the seat of the rocker and tack it in place using decorative upholstery tacks—one in each corner should be enough.

Illus. 96. Attach the seat to the rocker with upholstery tacks.

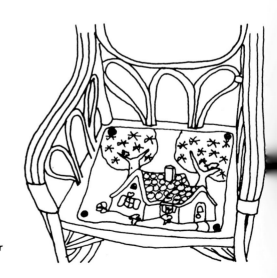

Lamp Shade

Here is an idea to brighten any room. Pick up a flower (as was done for the shade in Illus. 98) or other motif from a lamp's base and use it to decorate the lamp's shade. Start with either a completely finished lamp shade that you have made or one that you have bought ready-made. Be sure that the shade has two layers of fabric.

Prepare your design on paper as described on page 53. Place the paper face down on the *right* side of the lamp shade exactly where you want the design to be. Pin the paper in place, using as few pins as possible so you do not put too many holes in the fabric. Hold the lamp shade up to the light and trace the design onto the *wrong* side of the lamp shade. Remove the paper with the design on it.

Using either yarn or embroidery floss (depending on the delicacy of the design and the lamp shade), sew with a running stitch, all along the design. Then, go back over the stitching you just did, with a running stitch, going under where you went over and vice versa (see Illus. 76). Do *not* leave an opening as you did for the burlap catch-all on page 62.

Stuff this design by carefully poking a hole with any blunt-end instrument in the under fabric (bottom layer) of the lamp shade. The finer the fabric, the smaller the instrument you should use to poke the hole. Be careful not to break the threads. After stuffing with polyester fibre, close the hole by carefully coaxing the threads back together.

Illus. 97. Close-up of the flower on the lamp shade.

Illus. 99 (left). Even a child could make this delicate lamp for her own room.

Illus. 98 (right). A baby can always use an extra bib. Make a special one by adding a pleasing Trapunto design.

Illus. 100 (right). Make knee-padded Trapunto crawlers for your active little crawler!

Illus. 101 (left). Delicately hand stitch flowers for an adorable baby's dress.

Clothes for Your Children

Bib

Perk up a baby's bib with a cartoon animal, such as the duck in Illus. 102. Copy characters from children's coloring books or draw your own, and then make your own bib or decorate one that you have purchased. Terry cloth, used for the bib in Illus. 98, is a very good fabric for bibs because it is absorbent. A plastic liner also ensures extra cleanliness for a sloppy eater. (You may buy plastic by the yard in variety shops.)

If you have purchased a bib, you must first remove the binding (and, hence, the plastic liner) from round the edge. Now, for either a bought or hand-made bib, cut a piece of interfacing the same size as the bib and trace your design onto it. Stitch the design with yarn by hand. Stuff and then embroider any detail you would like on your animal. In Illus. 98, the eye and the beak were embroidered.

Replace the plastic liner on a bought bib or add plastic to a bib you made yourself. Baste all layers together. Using the binding foot on your sewing machine, carefully sew on binding (formally called single-fold bias tape) along the bib's edges using a color which complements your design.

Illus. 102. Hand stitching on a terry cloth bib makes particularly effective Tra punto. This is a close-up of the duck

Illus. 103. Close-up of the knee pad fish for the crawlers.

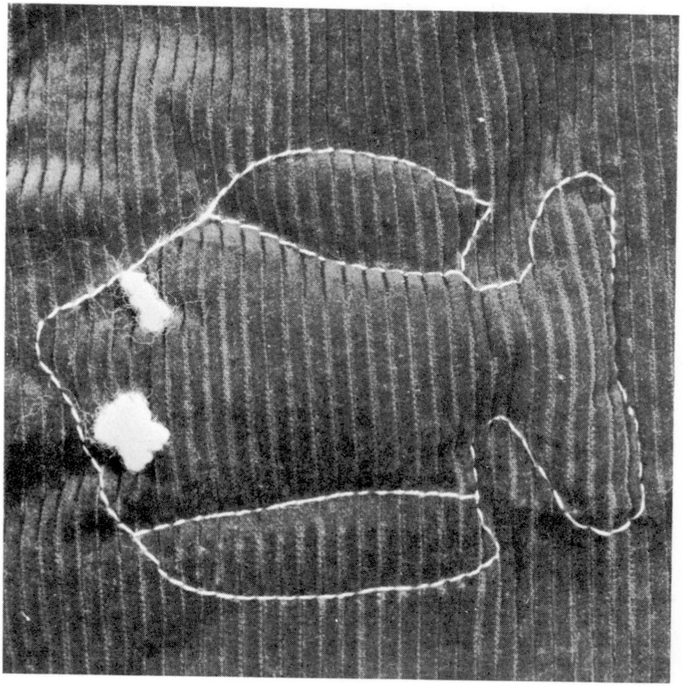

Crawlers

Make your child adorable knee pads to crawl about in that will be the talk of the baby world. Either buy or make a pair of crawlers like the ones in Illus. 100, preferably with a snap crotch which enables you to get inside the leg easily to work.

Apply a lively design to interfacing as described on page 53. Try the outfit on the child to mark where his knees are. Center the Trapunto design over this mark and pin it in place. Stitch on the machine, using buttonhole twist thread in the bobbin and the same color regular thread on the top. Set your machine for the longest stitch (six stitches per inch). Remember never to backtack. Leave an opening in the stitching through which to stuff. Embroider any necessary detail (see the eyes in Illus. 103).

Illus. 104. You will be elegant in a custom-made robe such as this one.

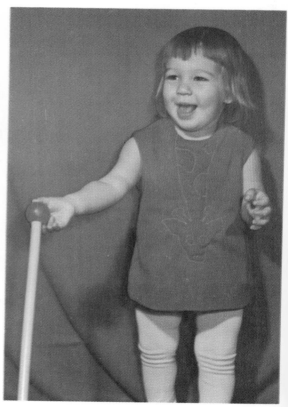

Illus. 105. Every little girl has a best-liked outfit— and this could surely be it. A simple Trapunto figure is all it takes.

Illus. 107 (left). You will be proud to carry your belongings anywhere—to work, to the store, to the beach—in this handy tote bag.

Illus. 106 (right). Draw a design and do Trapunto stitching before you add a hand-painted creation. Stuff when the paint is completely dry.

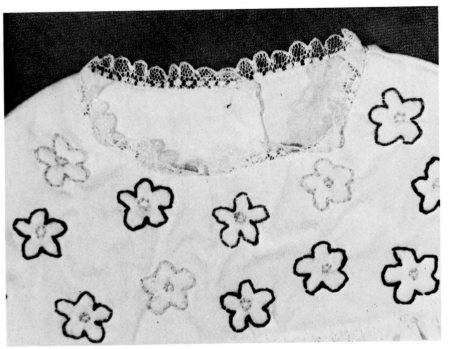

Illus. 108. Babies'
clothes are delightful
to create and decorate.
These simple flowers
change the entire
appearance of a plain
white dress.

Dresses

Baby's Dress

Dresses are wonderful clothes to adorn with Trapunto. For a baby, for example, you could add interest on the yoke of a dress that you bought or made. If the dress has a double-thickness yoke, like the one in Illus. 101, you do not need to use an additional layer of interfacing. If there is not a double-thickness yoke, however, cut a piece of interfacing the same size as the yoke. Transfer an original design onto the under-yoke or the interfacing. If you are using a separate piece of interfacing, attach it to the dress at this point by

tacking it, with the seam allowances tucked under, to all of the seam allowances of the dress at the neck, sleeves, shoulders and yoke.

Using small stitches, hand sew the design with embroidery floss. Stitch all the way around very small motifs, such as the flowers in Illus. 108.

Stuff by carefully poking a hole without breaking the threads, but do not stuff very small areas, such as the centers of these flowers. Close the holes in the interfacing or under-yoke by pushing the threads back together.

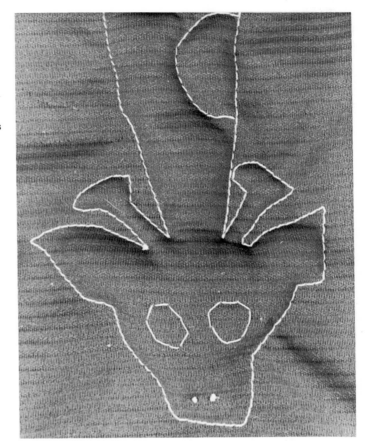

Child's Dress

When the baby grows older, she will certainly still love her outgrown Trapunto dress. Simply ask her to pick an animal and then reproduce it either at the center of a dress or at the neck, as the giraffe in Illus. 109. Follow the instructions for the crawlers on page 79.

And Now—

Elegance for Yourself!

Slippers

Here is your opportunity to make a pair of slippers to match a robe, nightgown, or lounging outfit.

Take an old pair of slippers apart carefully and use them for a pattern. Note how they were put together and use that information as a guide assembling your new slippers. Choose your fabrics wisely, so that your slippers will be machine washable and dryable. The outer fabric of the hand-made Trapunto slippers in Illus. 110 for example, is polyester double knit. The toe piece has a layer of interfacing for the Trapunto and the sole has interfacing for reinforcement.

Place your Trapunto design on the toe piece and finish the Trapunto before you begin to make the slippers. Follow the directions on page 54 for stuffing between two rows of stitching. (The rows of stitching in Illus. 111 are $\frac{1}{8}''$ apart.)

Pad the sole and toe piece with $\frac{1}{2}''$-thick foam rubber, which you can buy by the yard at variety shops.

After you have sewn all of the layers of the sole and the toe piece in place, using the original slipper construction as a guide, bind the edge with single-fold bias tape in a matching or contrasting color.

If the rubber sole from your old slippers is re-usable, you may use that to apply at this point. Otherwise, if you can find a sheet of rubber

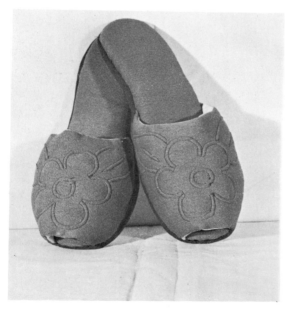

Illus. 110. Slippers with imaginative Trapunto on them are an original addition to anyone's wardrobe.

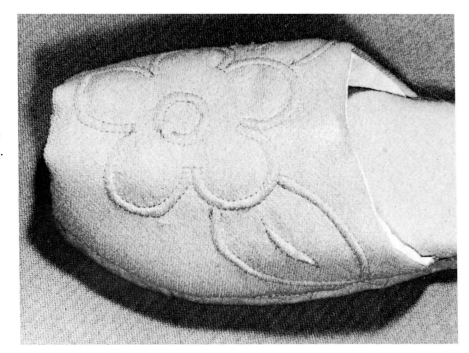

Illus. 111. Close-up of the slipper toe-piece.

heavy enough to be suitable for a sole, cut it to shape and sew it on. If you cannot find heavy rubber, ask your shoe repairman for help. If your home has stairs that are carpeted—or no stairs at all—it is not, in fact, necessary to have a rubber sole, which is actually merely a safety precaution.

Your hand-made slippers are now ready for wear.

Robe

Put a simple, yet elegant, Trapunto design on the hem and sleeves of a robe which you can make from a commercial pattern. The robe in Illus. 104 was made from a light-weight, fine silk satin. When you cut out your robe, be sure to allow for a $6\frac{1}{2}''$ hem. Completely make the garment—except for the hems in the sleeves and in the robe itself.

To make the Trapunto design in Illus. 112, fold up the hem allowance on the fold lines. Fold the raw edge under $\frac{1}{2}''$. Use buttonhole twist thread in the bobbin and regular thread of a matching color on top. With a ruler and a soft lead pencil, carefully and lightly score or mark your design onto the wrong side of the hem (after it has already been folded up). Stitch along all vertical lines. Estimate the amount of stuffing needed for each square and insert that amount into each vertical column.

When you have filled all of the bottom squares in this way, stitch along the first horizontal lines. Stuff the next row of squares up the column. When you have filled all of these squares, stitch along the next horizontal line. Repeat in this way until you have finished. The last line of stitching should catch the top edge of the hem.

When you have finished the Trapunto, go back and sew a pearl in the center of each square (see Illus. 112). Repeat the design on the sleeves.

You now have a lovely robe in which to entertain.

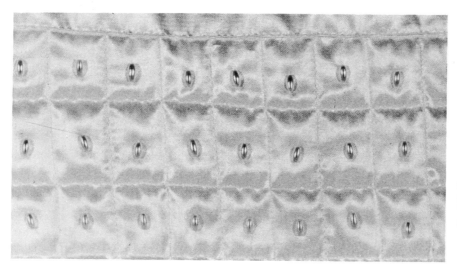

Illus. 112. Tiny pearls sewn into stuffed areas transform simple Trapunto into stylish elegance.

Long Skirt

Be right in style with a long evening skirt (Illus. 113). A border print especially lends itself to Trapunto. In the print in Illus. 113, only a few stripes are corded. They were chosen so that an over-all balanced look would result. Stuffing all of the stripes would be overwhelming.

Cut a piece of interfacing, using the skirt pattern. Make it as long as the border print is wide, allowing an extra half inch at the top. Place the selvage of the interfacing along the top of the print, if possible (see Illus. 114). When you cut out the skirt, allow 1″ extra in the length for the fabric that the Trapunto will take up.

Following the directions that accompany your pattern, make the skirt completely except for the hem. Next, sew the side seams of the interfacing. Placing the wrong sides together, pin the interfacing to the skirt so that the side seams match and the top edge of the interfacing is one half inch above the top stripe. (If this edge is not the selvage, it should be zig-zagged or pinked, to prevent ravelling.)

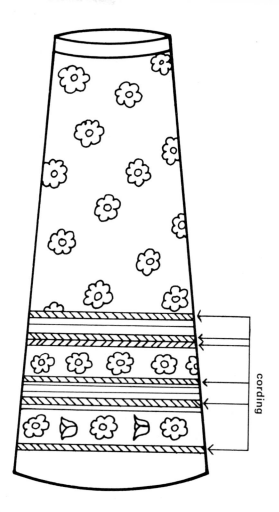

cording

Illus. 113. Use a fabric with a border print for an elegant, unusual evening skirt.

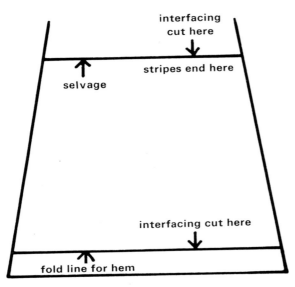

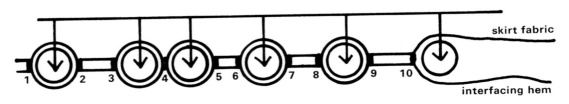

interfacing
cut here

stripes end here

selvage

interfacing cut here

fold line for hem

Illus. 114. Cut interfacing as shown here.

Use regular thread in a color that will show the least. Stitch through both thicknesses, from the right side, starting at the top. Insert cording, which you can buy at a sewing shop, starting at the center back seam. Push it firmly up against the row of the stitching that you just made. Stitch the next row, and all of the others, with your zipper foot on the right side of the needle (see Illus. 115). When stitching the cording in place, pull the fabric to the right, so that it looks like the zipper foot will run over the cording. (It will not.) This keeps the cording taut and wrinkle-free (see Illus. 116). Cut the cording at the end of each row so that the ends butt (meet) and do not overlap.

Since the stripes are of various widths, use various weights of cording. The best method of choosing the correct weight cording for your stripes is trial and error.

skirt fabric

1 2 3 4 5 6 7 8 9 10

interfacing hem

Illus. 115. Stitch along the top of the stripes before you insert cording, following the order of the numbers in the cross-section above.

If your skirt ends up too short, do not worry. You can lengthen it to within $\frac{1}{2}''$ of the raw edge. Buy hem facing and attach it to the raw edge of the hem with a $\frac{1}{4}''$ seam allowance. Press both seam allowances towards the hem facing. Stitch as shown in Illus. 117. (This is called under-stitching.) Press the hem facing up, so that the seam is $\frac{1}{4}''$ from the fold. Hem as usual, catching only the interfacing, not the right side of the fabric.

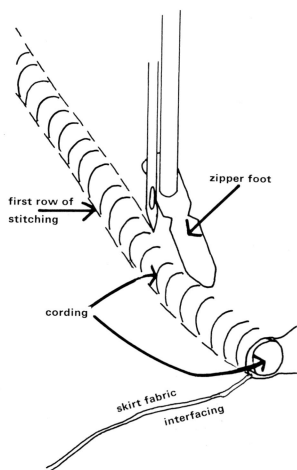

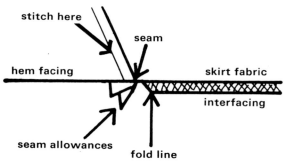

Illus. 117. To lengthen a skirt, add hem facing to the raw edge of the hem and stitch as shown above.

Tote Bag

Carry your handiwork from place to place in a lovely tote bag (like the one on the front cover) made of burlap, which is easy to work with. Use a commercial pattern for a tote bag or decorate a ready-made fabric one.

Cut a piece of interfacing the size of the front of the bag. Transfer the design as you did for the afghan (see page 56). Stitch the design on the machine, using regular thread in a color that matches the fabric. Leave a 1″ opening for stuffing,

Illus. 118. Close-up of the flower on the tote bag pictured on the front cover and on page 81.

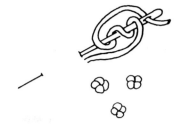

as you did on the afghan. Stuff and close the opening. Notice in Illus. 118 that lines of stitching through the centers of the flower petals and on the leaves give the impression of veins. Stuff the flower stems with yarn threaded on a tapestry needle (see page 54).

Outline all areas by hand with a running stitch of brightly colored yarn, except for the flower and leaf veins. You do not need to go back over the running stitch with a second running stitch as before (see page 62), because you did that only to add strength. In this project, you ensured strength by the machine stitching. Decorate the flower centers with French knots. To make a French knot, bring a threaded needle through the fabric, wind the thread or yarn round the tip of the needle and re-insert the needle near to the same spot. Pull the thread or yarn taut and a French knot appears (see Illus. 119).

Assemble the tote bag according to the instructions that come with the pattern. Line the bag. To do this, cut out two pieces of lining fabric the same size as the front and back of the tote bag. Assemble the lining as you did the bag itself. With the wrong sides together (the tote bag is right side out), insert the lining inside the tote bag. Tack the two pieces together.

Purse

Make a suede fringed purse for yourself or your daughter. Buy cotton suede by the yard or cut up an old vest, using the fringe on the bottom of the vest for the bottom of the purse.

Up to now, you have mostly depended on your chosen fabric and thread or yarn for color. A most effective and rewarding alternative method is to paint a design onto the fabric and then do Trapunto round the design. The sailboat on the purse in Illus. 106 was hand-painted.

To make your purse, cut one piece of suede so that the fringe will be at the bottom (see Illus. 120). Allow $\frac{5}{8}''$ seam allowances on each side and $1\frac{1}{2}''$ on top. Cut a piece of suede for the back exactly like the piece for the front. Then, cut a 2″-wide strip of suede for the handle, making it as long as you like.

Do Trapunto before you paint the design and before you sew the purse together. Cut interfacing the size of the body of the purse (minus the fringe). Trace the design onto the interfacing. Using thread of a matching color, stitch by machine, leaving an opening, as described on page 57, for the larger areas you will stuff. For smaller areas, such as the flag and the wave in Illus. 106, stitch, leaving no openings.

The next step is the painting. Special tubes of paint are used for liquid embroidery (available in variety and needlecraft shops); follow the manufacturer's instructions. When the paint is completely dry, stuff according to the instructions on page 57 (with an opening) and page 75 (without an opening).

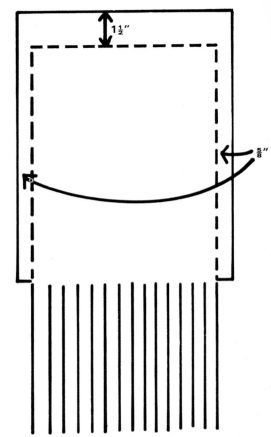

Illus. 120. Cut suede for a fringed purse as shown above.

Place the right sides of the purse together and stitch the side seams. Turn the purse right side out. Top stitch across the bottom, just above the fringe. Use buttonhole twist thread in the bobbin

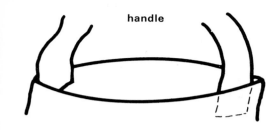

handle

Illus. 121. With the purse right side out, place the handle inside as indicated here and pin.

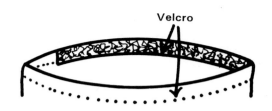

Velcro

Illus. 122. Insert Velcro along the inside top edge of the purse, leaving a small space for your finger.

and on top of the machine. Sew the handle together by folding it in half lengthwise, with the right side on the inside, and then by stitching along the length. Do not sew the ends together. Turn the handle right side out. Turn down the top edge of the purse. Place one end of the handle on the back top edge of the purse and place the other end on the front top edge on the opposite side (see Illus. 121). Pin the handle in place. Insert Velcro—a material which sticks to itself and is often used for closings—inside the top edges for a closure, putting it as close to the side seam as you can, leaving a space for your finger at one end (see Illus. 122). By machine, stitch the Velcro in place all the way round, even where there is no Velcro. This results in even top stitching on the right side, which is even prettier if you use buttonhole twist in the bobbin.

Use the suggestions and ideas in this book to develop exciting Trapunto projects of your own. Do not be bashful about adding your own ideas to the projects presented here. Have fun!

Index

ACKNOWLEDGMENTS

Author Linda S. Weeks would like to thank the following people from Tennessee for contributing quilts for the Patchwork Section of this book: Mrs. Annie Stanley of Woodville; Mrs. Lucille Lane of Woodville; Mrs. Parks (Mama Goldie) of Nutbush; Dana Parks of Nutbush; Mrs. Russell Jackocks of Woodville and Lou Ann Camp of Halls. Author Jo Ippolito Christensen would like to thank the following people for their co-operation and willingness in making Trapunto projects: Sonie Ashner, Karol Dyer, Sharon Hanlon, Betty Hills, Carol Hoadley, Jane Keady, Zekiye Miller, Diane Pearsall, Pat Regan, Jaci Reuter, Evelyn Shoemaker, Melanie Shuter and Pegi Stallings. Thanks also to Zekiye Miller, Claire Anne Powell and Mandy Reuter for posing for photographs.